THE LATINO GUIDE
TO CREATING
FAMILY HISTORIES

A HANDBOOK FOR
STUDENTS, PARENTS & TEACHERS
PLUS THE TOP 350 HISPANIC SURNAMES

BY AMBASSADOR
JULIAN NAVA

SPECIAL RESEARCH BY KIRK WHISLER

WPR BOOKS: LATINO INSIGHTS
CARLSBAD, CA

THE BOOK CREATION TEAM

Cover & Interior Photographs: From the Julian Nava family
Publisher & Part 5 Author: Kirk Whisler

For more about books presented by WPR Publishing, please go to www. WPRbooks.com.

WPR BOOKS: Latino Insights
3445 Catalina Dr., Carlsbad, CA 92010-2856
www.WPRbooks.com   760-434-1223   kirk@whisler.com

This book is dedicated to my mother because she always told me as one of eight children about her family, life and times in old Mexico. Her stories shaped my life and gave it strength. She and my father were pioneers and this helped me want to do news things and see far away places.

Julian Nava

Julian Nava and mother Ruth at Pomona College graduation in 1951. She could not understand ceremony in English.

Table of Contents

FORWARD

Each of us is a part of history – our family history, our church and school history, our community and national history, and even international history.

Professor and Ambassador Julian Nava has provided us with *The Latino Guide to Creating Family Histories*. This text will help you develop your family history, as well as answer the important question, "Where did I come from and where am I going."

It was a pleasure to serve as Superintendent of the Los Angeles Unified School District during Dr. Nava's tenure as a school board member and President. He was elected at-large in a district with an estimated population of 3.4 million people, 719 square miles, 706 schools, 82,000 employees, and an enrollment of 735,000 students. Dr. Nava provided extraordinary leadership as a board member and President. He served 12 years from 1967-1979.

This book is an excellent example of his awareness of the importance of family to shaping young minds for the future ahead.

William Johnston

Superintendent, Los Angeles Unified School District, 1971-1981

INTRODUCTION

As a teacher and school administrator for many years I have seen first hand the importance of family backgrounds in shaping young minds and spirits. Family history shapes all of us, and the more we know about our family history, the better we are.

As principal of two junior highs that were racially and economically mixed with several hundred adolescents being bussed from different parts of the city, taunting, picking on each other: racial slurs were too frequent. Several English, Science, and History teachers on my staff focused on the positive contributions of each youth's culture, values, mannerisms, and home experiences. Much of this may have been absent at home.

A most satisfying experience for this teacher/principal professor was teaching "Adolescent Youth" at California State University at Northridge. One activity that all students participated in was to identify their religious preferences. I scheduled visits to the different churches, temples and other places of worship. After the visits we tried to surmise why their parents or ancestors chose their special way of life and how this might have shaped their personality.

My grandmother, Cuca, encouraged me by sharing stories about my ancestors in Mexico. These stories helped me know about who I am and where I come from.

Ed Moreno

SPECIAL INTRODUCTION

I was born in a mining camp in Miami, Arizona, during the Great Depression. My father, a Mexican copper miner, was deported with many others to Mexico…I never saw him again. I was only three years old.

My mother and grandmother raised me through those hard years during the depression. Telling me to be strong and resourceful, they said, "Be proud of your Mexican heritage, learn English, but *never* forget your Spanish". We eventually moved to California and settled in East Los Angeles, where I went to local schools and graduated from Garfield High. I joined the U.S. Army. As a veteran of the Korean War, I went to college under the G.I. Bill.

I worked for the Chrysler Motor Company and joined the United Auto Workers Union (UAW). My English and Spanish were a benefit, because I was promoted as a UAW International Representative for Latin American and Carribean Affairs.

My family, friends, and community were great supporters of my progress. I used my language and organizing skills to work in politics and as a result President

Jimmy Carter appointed me as the U.S. Ambassador to the United Nations Educational, Scientific, and Cultural Organization (UNESCO) in Paris France.

While in France with UNESCO I discovered that my great grandfather had migrated to California during the 1848 gold rush. He married a Mexican citizen, since California was then part of Mexico.

With my world travels and family discoveries I have learned of my roots. This has given me a greater meaning as to who I am and strengthened my cultural traditions and self esteem.

Discover your roots.

Congressman Esteban Torres,
Retired

Insights

We are all born with a past, inherited, absorbed, and assimilated into who we are. When circumstances remove individuals from their own nation or tribe, self-discovery becomes more complex and confusing. Of Mexican heritage, with Spanish as my first language, my grammar school experience in the 1940's in a Russian Jewish barrio in East L.A. was frequently bewildering and sometimes upsetting. It wasn't just language; I could not understand the relationships which my classmates had with their parents, and the teacher, very different from what was expected of me.

When I started gathering family history, I quickly realized we Mexican heritage individuals were either invisible, or maligned in history. I concluded, the only way for our story to be told correctly was for us to tell it.

Our ancestors brought us to the present through tremendous sacrifice and courage. Identifying the challenges our ancestors faced will reveal their character and the inherent potential within each of us. We honor the memory of our parents and grandparents by sharing who they were, their trials, their strengths, their talents. Nothing has empowered me more as an individual then knowing the facts of my heritage. We can view the future with boldness and with confidence.

Dr. Julian Nava's manual on including family history in the classroom is quite important and timely. The United States is experiencing a collision of cultures like never before. Successful adjustments to these social changes will be facilitated by each individual knowing the history of his own extended family. Family history knowledge is a priceless gift . . . better than gold.

We cannot ignore our past and expect to understand the present.

Historical exclusion is historical confusion,

Mimi Lozano

www.SomosPrimos.com

PREFACE

Enclosed you will find four handbooks bound together and a teacher's guide to help students and others to write their family history. The teacher's handbook offers suggestions on how to relate and enrich the regular curriculum. Handbooks for students and parents in both English and Spanish help develop this school activity that holds life-long benefits.

This project focuses on living relatives, family friends and public records at hand or on the web. The depth and breath of family research will depend on motivations and skills.

Family genealogy beyond present times is increasingly available from web sources like "Ancestry.com," or Mormon Church genealogical centers locally or in Salt Lake City. This is beyond the scope of the handbooks, however.

For example, the Nava family name first comes from a small coastal region of northern Spain from where the first Nava came to the New World in 1519, Spanish records show. Since the heir to the Spanish throne has the title of Principe de Asturias, this odd fact inspired me to visit the region and just look around. Many family genealogies may hold similar surprises in documents, photos and personal accounts.

Only a few pages of family history can start a personal hobby or adventure, becoming a treasure for one's children and their children, holding information they could not gather. Both school learning and personal growth can result from starting one's family history.

The Nava famly photos and one document enclosed throughout the book are examples of what you may gather about your family.

Julián Nava

Ambassador Nava and wife Patricia signing documents in front of U.S. Embassy Building in Mexico City in 1979.

Part One of the Book

THE STUDENT GUIDE TO CREATING FAMILY HISTORIES

Chapter 1
YOUR FAMILY HISTORY

This handbook will help you discover the history of your family. You can do this by using the suggestions and charts in this handbook. If your school has computers to help you, this information may be put into a computer bank of information. When you put information into a computer memory bank you may print your family history whenever you like and compare it with information about other students that many share your family names far away. Perhaps you have relatives in other cities, states and countries that you did not know about.

You may use this handbook to uncover your family history, even if your school does not have a computer. Simply organize the information you receive and keep a diary of important information.

To start this journey of discovery, you will find that the materials in this book will help you list your parents, brothers and sisters as well as other relatives you know. Gradually, you can add new names as you discover relatives and ancestors farther back in time.

Perhaps many of you will form a family and have

children of your own. The beginning of your family history can be passed on to future generations and they can add to the family history. Your efforts can start a family tradition of your own.

In **Part Two: Creating the Family Tree Workbook** of this book (see side tabs) of this handbook you will find charts for use in tracing your family history. We recommend that you make copies of these charts for your personal use, rather than writing in the book, and that you follow the instructions in the handbook.

Julian Nava as pall bearer for Cesear Chavez funeral in 1993.

Chapter 2
AN INTRODUCTION TO THE SEARCH FOR FAMILY ROOTS

All of us wonder about the past and the future. Sooner or later, everyone asks the common question, where did we come from and where we are going? What we know today is made up of what happened to us before. We are all historians because we look back and try to learn from our experiences. Our learning and experiences make up our memory. We remember things that happened to us and learn from them. When we have happy memories about something, we want more of the same. Most of our present thinking is made up of past memories. Since we look to the future as well as the past, we might say that each of us lives in three time zones: the past, present and future.

We all want different things and we set out to obtain them. Everyone shares basic needs like eating, sleeping and being near loved ones. When we make plans we shape the future, like our parents have done before us. Our own life is like one link in a long chain. This long chain is the history of our family, and its many generations before us. Everyone has a long family history and we are made richer by knowing about our family's past.

Have you ever asked questions like the following?

- ✔ Why do I look like some relatives and not like others?

- ✔ Why do some things interest me, and not others?

- ✔ How come I can do some things easier than others?

- ✔ Why are some people so different?

Questions like these show us the need to understand our origins and ourselves.

The time comes when we decide to become something in particular. We want to become like those we admire. It is very natural to change our goals from time to time, by the way. Sometimes our parents may want us to become something they believe is good and other times they leave such decisions to us. All of these experiences are part of our planning our life. Rather than just drift into the future we can look back, evaluate our experiences and then point ourselves in the direction we want to go. What we are depends greatly on the characteristics our family has given to us. That is why we look like them.

Our family characteristics have a source much farther back than our own parents, however. Each of our two parents had their own mother and father. Each of our four grandparents had their own mother and father, giving us eight great-grandparents. If we trace our family back far enough we each have hundreds of ancestors. We have genes or characteristics of some ancestors and not others. Perhaps your parents have said something like, "My, you laugh just like your uncle," or "You have your grandmother's eyes." Indeed, our shape or personality may come from ancestors our parents know nothing about.

We are the present chapter of a long family history. As we discover more about our family's history we learn more about ourselves. This new knowledge can help us decide what to do with our future. We shape our future with the decisions we make every day.

Uncovering our family history can be a very exciting project because family members have had happy and sad experiences, successes and failures. By sharing what we discover, we will be offering a very special gift to friends and our own descendants. Our children, and their children, will remember and become stronger from what we have done.

You may use this handbook to begin to uncover your family history. Using a few simple steps you will collect important information and organize it using a set of simple charts.

STUDENT GUIDE

Chapter 3
HOW TO USE THIS HANDBOOK

Your family history starts with you. The information in this Handbook contains everything you need to search for your family history as far back as your living relatives or information about deceased ones if it is available.

This handbook will help you without depending on the use of computers for research. However, if you attend a school that has a computer available for student use you can search for computer banks of information for deeper research. Of course, you can use a computer for writing, storing your information and sending it through the web. Your teacher may help you in all this.

Numerous groups have already placed family names into computer databases that serve as a library. Some of these collections have the names of millions of individuals, and their family relations, going back centuries. Such genealogical study is not the object of this Handbook, however.

This Handbook can help you whether or not a computer is available. The Handbook is low tech, we might say, The information in this Handbook contains everything you need to search for your family history as far back as your living relatives, deceased ones or information gained from family friends. You can do this yourself. This is the beginning of your family history, which you can give as a Christmas gift or for a birthday present. As time goes by such a gift will be more valuable to the receiver because such a personal gift could not be purchased at a bookstore.

The various charts found in **Part Two: Creating the Family Tree Workbook** will help you gather the information you need. You can make copies of some charts to distribute to persons with information you seek.

Nava with Presidential Military inspection team under President Ronald Reagan

STUDENT GUIDE

Chapter 4
FINDING INFORMATION FOR YOUR FAMILY HISTORY

Let us give some attention to how you might gather information for your family history. Little by little you will find out more information, as you become a detective about your family history. Identifying the names on your family's ancestors may require help.

Your parents will help you with information for the family chart. Each one knows the names of their parents, of course, and probably the names of their grandparents. They may not know the second family name of their parents and their grandparents, however. In the United States we inherited a custom from England where only the married man's name is used for the children in the family. At this point you will have to start being a detective. Look around for help wherever you can find it.

One method for getting information is to talk or write to your uncles and other older relatives for family names and events. Send them a copy of the family chart and ask them to help fill in the blanks. Suggest that they write to you with details or stories about the names they add. Photographs or copies of interesting documents will also be good. In this way, your family history can begin to take form.

If your class makes this a project, then you can discuss other ways to gather this information with your teacher. Work with your classmates and friends. You can gather many good ideas working together with others.

There are several government agencies that will help you in the search for your family history. Every city or county in the United States is required by law to keep birth and death records. Perhaps your parents or relatives have some of these records at home. If your family came from another country, the search may be more difficult, but all governments try to keep records of their people. Usually you can find a lot of information by writing letters. Your parents will help you in this effort. Your local church may help also. Talk to your minister, priest, or rabbi. Some religious groups, such as the Mormons, keep excellent records of family names wherever they can all over the world. You may want to gain their help. You do not have to be a Mormon to make use of their records.

Here we have a list of some of the most obvious sources of information, starting from the simple and going to the more complex:

FAMILY SOURCES

(talk or write to these);

✔ Your parents

✔ Brothers and sisters

✔ Grandparents on both sides of the family

✔ Uncles and aunts

✔ Cousins

Church Records

Marriage, baptismal and death records are usually kept for many years (even centuries). Computer files of this information are becoming more common.

Local Government Offices

Marriage, birth and death records are commonly found in the location where the event took place. Cities, counties and states usually have these records. They are open to the public.

Other Local Sources

Public libraries have books on local biographies, or accounts of past events. Books on places far away can sometimes be borrowed through the local library. Commentaries can be helpful also.

National Government Sources

✔ Military service records contain considerable information for individuals who served in the armed forces.

✔ Application records for residence or citizenship are also very rich sources of information.

✔ Social Security records may help you find information since the 1930's to the present.

✔ National archives go back almost 200 years. Your teacher or local librarian may help you identify other national government sources of information.

✔ Online you can find family ancestry records at www.ancestry.com and other websites.

As you can see, much help is available to you depending upon how far back in time and how deeply you want to dig into your heritage. That is your decision to make. Family sources and friends make a good start.

STUDENT GUIDE

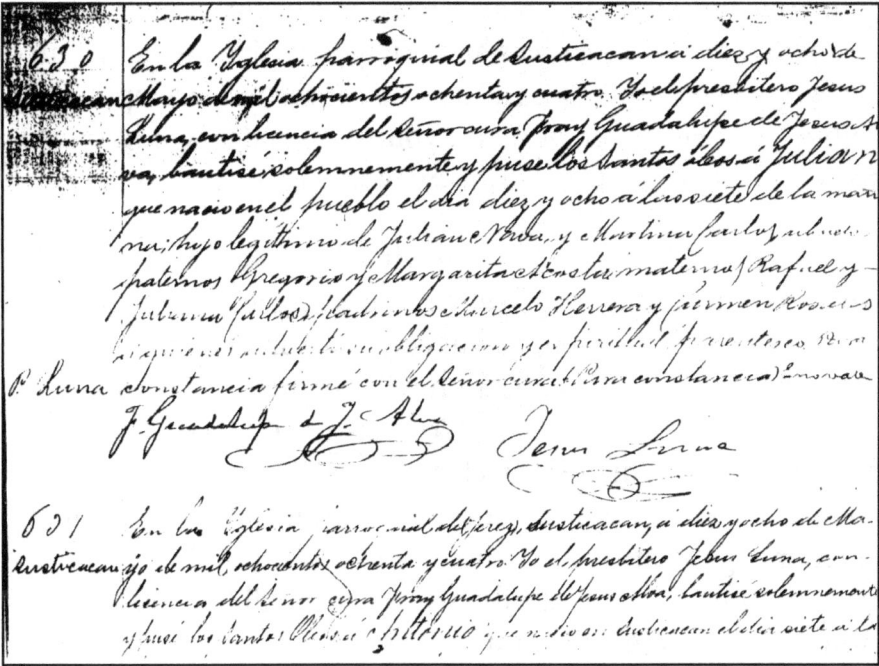

Parrochial church record of Ambassador Nava's father Julian's birth record from 1884.

Chapter 5
WORKING WITH YOUR SCHOOL

Your teachers can be of great help to you in searching into your family's past. Starting with your immediate family you will also have relatives and friends to give you assistance. Local government offices and national records are open for public use. However, you and your classmates will find ways to get much of the work done by working together in class.

Your teacher can help you with the practical steps towards getting started. You will be doing activities that are part of the curriculum, but are now directed towards a personal interest. Your search will be greatly helped when one of your classes undertakes the to work on family histories as a group. Many class activities can be planned, such as field trips to local sources of information. Parent and teacher organizations may get involved as well. When you show interest in your family history you will be surprised how many people will want to help you. In fact your interest may well get them started on their own family history as well.

You may find that your family history has some fascinating chapters. Almost all families have had some happy or sad events take place, as well as exciting or tragic episodes. You will want to write down some of these stories, or make oral reports to your class. Public speaking is a very useful ability to develop. Everything that you do can be preserved for your children and relatives when you record your work in a computer. You too become part of history. Your descendants can add to what you have accomplished as part of an endless story.

Nava pounding on Berlin Wall just days after liberation in 1989.

Chapter 6
WRITING A HISTORY OF YOUR FAMILY

You can start this history with what you learn about your parents and other relatives. Later, you will find out more information to add in later years. But you will be the one who " started the ball rolling". To start, how do we go from information you gather to an essay or a short book?

Using the charts in **Part Two: Creating the Family Tree Workbook** of this book (see side tabs) for the information you gather, the writings will be organized in a natural manner. Use a separate sheet for each person you talk to or communicate with. This technique will help in composing your essay. You may spread out the sheets on a table or the floor. The sequence for writing your essay starts to take shape as you see your raw material before you. Gaps or missing information become apparent. You may find that some important things are unknown or kept secret from you for one reason or another. It is up to you to decide what to do in these cases. Maybe you too have some secrets.

With the help of your teacher you can start to write a short book about your family history. Some books are long and others are short, but they all have three parts: a

Beginning, Middle and an End. It's that simple.

In the Beginning, you can include a title page, an introduction and a table of contents. Look at your own Student Manual to see what we mean. Your introduction tells the reader what you are going to write about, how you are going to do it, and maybe why you are writing the book. The table of contents tells about the parts of the book. The MIDDLE of the book is where you do what you said you were going to do in the introduction. Here you include what you have learned about your family history. The END of the book is sometimes called a conclusion. Here you make some final remarks for the reader that summarizes the contents of the book or gives a final impression.

The charts in **Part Two: Creating the Family Tree Workbook** will help you gather information. Use the charts as they are or adapt them to suit your needs. Anything goes as long as it helps you. For example, you might record personal interviews. In later years you may be able to add information, photos or documents, your family history will be a living thing you are giving life to by using this manual.

STUDENT GUIDE

Chapter 7
USING COMPUTERS FOR YOUR FAMILY HISTORY

You may start to write you family history by using the charts in **Part Two: Creating the Family Tree Workbook** of this book (see side tabs). Computers are useful in several ways, however. Of course, they are useful for writing, and storage of the material you have written. You may preserve a copy of your writing for adding to later. By e-mail you could send your writing almost anywhere.

Various groups in the United States and abroad are creating collections of names, dates and families in computer databases. Each year many thousands of names are added to the millions already recorded. In time just about everyone alive now and in the past may be listed. The Mormon Church has collected one of the largest databases for family names, but governments and other private groups do the same thing. To connect with these groups the Internet, web, or groups like AOL or Google are available via your computer.

Many individuals have discovered lost or unknown

relatives by a comparison of surnames on both sides of the family with other similar surnames found in locations where your relatives lived. Using computers you may find a needle in a haystack. Perhaps you are related to a famous person in the past, or perhaps a rascal.

This manual does not depend on computers except for word processing, storage and transmission through e-mail. You can start your family history low tech, so to speak. Your family history can go as far back as living relatives and friends with great detail. Later on you may find interesting information by means of computer databases going back several centuries.

Your family history is more than a simple genealogy, which deals with parentage going back many generations.. History is what your parents and ancestors actually did or what has happened to them. You may want to know how your ancestors lived and what life was like at the time. You can find out many things about living conditions in times past by reading books about where your ancestors lived. However, the beginning of your family history is the collection of information facilitated by use of the enclosed charts.

Chapter 8
HOW TO USE YOUR FAMILY HISTORY

The family history you have compiled is for your personal use. You may choose to start a family archive. Your children or other family members may want to have copies of this archive and perhaps add to it. The history you have gathered will help tell who you are and where you came from. Of course, you are only starting an effort that may take a longer than you have in this school semester. But you will have started the effort and can continue the search later on your own.

Perhaps you may use your family history for class work in a subsequent semester. Study in fields like geography, economics and politics can shed light on your family history and supply information for adding to your story. Some students in college are writing their family histories also. Their work approaches book length. Your work can be a beginning.

You will find that relatives you have contacted for information will be curious about your discoveries. After all you will have more information than any one of those you have contacted. Probably you have devoted more time to this search than most of your relatives, including your parents. Therefore you will have a very special person in your family,

You alone have a special gift for all of your loved ones. You can make copies of your family history and give them for birthday or Christmas presents. If you gather other information about ancestors, then your family history will be an even richer and more interesting record. Perhaps you will discover a hero in your past, or a painter, inventor or even a bandit! The United States is a land of immigrants and many have surprising stories to tell. You can never tell what you will find now that you have started the search.

Julian's mother and seven Nava children at beach in Long Beach in 1935. The future ambassador is in the white shirt.

Part Two of the Book

Creating The Family Tree Workbook

Put a family photo here

INTRODUCTION

This part is the heart of the book - where you do the research and write the answers you get from family members and your research. Please keep in mind that this is a first step in discovering your family. Please keep in mind that you want to eventually use this information to go back more generations. It will also give you something many of your relatives will find useful and interesting.

CREATING THE FAMILY TREE

CHART #1
BASIC INFORMATION ABOUT THE STUDENT

This chart contains information about the student compiling his/her family history.

STUDENT'S NAME _____

Date of birth _____

City & Country of birth _____

Present address

_____

_____

Languages spoken _____

Current grade in school: _____

Favorite subjects in school:

Favorite hobbies:

Favorite sports:

Put Picture Here

of Yourself

Chart #2
MY FAMILY TREE

These charts bring together the genealogy together back to the parents, grandparents, key aunts, uncles and cousins.

FATHER

Name/*Nombre:* _____

Date of birth: _____

City/County: _____

Languages spoken: _____

Career: _____

Hobbies: _____

Put Picture Here

of your Father

MOTHER

Name/*Nombre:* _____

Date of birth: _____

City/County: _____

Languages spoken: _____

Career: _____

Hobbies: _____

CREATING THE FAMILY TREE

Put Picture Here

of your Mother

Maternal Grandmother

My mother's mother

Name/*Nombre:* _____

Date of birth: _____

City/County: _____

Languages spoken: _____

Career: _____

Hobbies: _____

Date of death: _____

Put Picture Here
of your Grandmother

MATERNAL GRANDFATHER

My mother's father

Name/*Nombre*: _____

Date of birth: _____

City/County: _____

Languages spoken: _____

Career: _____

Hobbies: _____

Date of death: _____

CREATING THE FAMILY TREE

Put Picture Here

of your Grandfather

41

PATERNAL GRANDMOTHER

My father's mother

Name/*Nombre*: _____

Date of birth: _____

City/County: _____

Languages spoken: _____

Career: _____

Hobbies: _____

Date of death: _____

Put Picture Here

of this Grandmother

PATERNAL GRANDFATHER

My father's father

Name/*Nombre:* _____

Date of birth: _____

City/County: _____

Languages spoken: _____

Career: _____

Hobbies: _____

Date of death: _____

CREATING THE FAMILY TREE

Put Picture Here

of this Grandfather

A FAVORITE AUNT

Name/*Nombre*: _____

Date of birth: _____

City/County: _____

Languages spoken: _____

Career: _____

Hobbies: _____

Put Picture Here

of this Aunt

A FAVORITE AUNT

Name/*Nombre:* _____

Date of birth: _____

City/County: _____

Languages spoken: _____

Career: _____

Hobbies: _____

CREATING THE FAMILY TREE

Put Picture Here

of this Aunt

A Favorite Uncle

Name/*Nombre:* _____

Date of birth: _____

City/County: _____

Languages spoken: _____

Career: _____

Hobbies: _____

Put Picture Here

of this Uncle

A FAVORITE UNCLE

Name/*Nombre:* _____

Date of birth: _____

City/County: _____

Languages spoken: _____

Career: _____

Hobbies: _____

CREATING THE FAMILY TREE

Put Picture Here

of this Uncle

A FAVORITE COUSIN

Name/*Nombre:* _____

Date of birth: _____

City/County: _____

Languages spoken: _____

Career: _____

Hobbies: _____

Put Picture Here

of this Cousin

A FAVORITE COUSIN

Name/*Nombre*: _____

Date of birth: _____

City/County: _____

Languages spoken: _____

Career: _____

Hobbies: _____

CREATING THE FAMILY TREE

Put Picture Here

of this Cousin

Chart #3
QUESTIONS FOR PARENTS

These are sample questions. Write down responses or make use of a voice recorder. More than one interview may be necessary for maximum results. Some parents may be sensitive about some of these questions. Use your judgment about how to proceed to gain parental confidence. Other persons may have information about your parents.

Where was each of your parents born? Are there any birth or baptismal certificates available to copy?

What was their family like? How many brothers and sisters did they have? Write down the names.

What did each of your parents do before they married? Where did they go to school, for example?

How did your parents happen to meet? Which one saw the other first?

How did your parents decide to become a couple or marry?

How was the new couple formed? Did the families of your parents take part in the selection or did your parents choose each other?

Where did your parents marry (city, state or country)?

What was the marriage ceremony like (various religious groups have their own customs about wedding ceremonies)? Was the marriage among family only or were there friends present? Was it a small or large wedding? Was there a party or reception after the wedding? Are there copies of wedding photos available for your project?

What do your parents want for your future?

Part Three of the Book
THE PARENT GUIDE TO CREATING FAMILY HISTORIES

Chapter 1
OUR FAMILY HISTORY

Perhaps your children have come home from school with questions about their family history. All this may be new, pleasant or annoying. They may ask for old family photos and documents, perhaps trips to libraries or offices of public records.

All this stems from a school project called " My Family History."

This project is important for the student. Your assistance is vital.

Every family has a unique history of course. Young people are often ignorant about their family history beyond their immediate family unit, however. Children wonder about why things are as they are. This uncertainty can lead to feelings of isolation. Parents may feel that some information can be shared later. This is a parent's right to judge. Sharing information with prudence earlier rather than later can strengthen family bonds. This project can also preserve colorful family stories before they are lost.

PARENT GUIDE

Chapter 2
AN INTRODUCTION FOR PARENTS HELPING THEIR CHILDREN TO WRITE THEIR FAMILY HISTORY

The handbook has three parts: a Students Manual, a Teachers Manual, and a Parents Manual. The three components are keyed together to facilitate coordination. Parents can help their student with activities at home, or help students contact relatives and family friends. The record is clear that students learn much more when the family and community join into the learning process.

Students develop more personal responsibility when they discover fascinating elements in their past. They discover how they fit into the community, nation and world. Subjects like geography, economics, culture and history come to life in a personally meaningful manner. By learning about the life of great-grand parents, when possible, the entire globe becomes part of their family reality. After all, we are a land of immigrants and family history research brings this to light in a personal way for the student.

Chapter 3
HANDS-ON HELP FOR ONE'S CHILDREN

A family conversation about the project can list the ways in which parents can help. Since both the student and parent manual use the same charts, familiarity with these is a good start. Parents may want their own time to gather some of the information sought in the charts. For example, a list of relatives and friends for the student to contact would be helpful. Perhaps parent calls or letters to some contacts would pave the way for student research.

It may be helpful for the student to talk with parents separately although joint sessions may be better. It is possible that information may emerge that is new to one parent or the other.

Family records or documents may have to be dug up. It's a good time to make copies of such material for safer keeping.

Joint visits to relatives or friends can be helpful. Some of these may have other leads to contribute, as well as tips about newspapers, etc. All these add to the start of the research project.

The student project may well become a family enterprise

Nava family crest from Asturias, Spain

Chapter 4
FINDING SOURCES OF INFORMATION

Parents, relatives near and far, as well as family friends will be the initial sources of information. Students can be encouraged to write to distant relatives and sources. This contact will make for stronger bonds. If a language other than English is necessary, then new abilities will be strengthened.

Here is a list of sources for you to discuss with your student:

✔ Family sources

✔ Friends and neighbors

✔ Church records- your own church or a local Mormon church will help entry into their computer archive of family records. These are open to everyone.

✔ County and state office records are open to the public

✔ National records like immigration,

citizenship and military service

This detective work can be the start of a life-long endeavor. It is very likely the student can make additions over time, especially when the first efforts are recorded in a computer for safekeeping.

Nava family at Lienzo Charro he helped organize

Chapter 5
WORKING WITH THE SCHOOL

Parental involvement in the family history project is vital to the success of the pupil. In addition, few things can strengthen family bonds as exploring family history together. How can parental involvement take place?

Simple encouragement for the project is a good start. Responses to the student's questions may be limited by personal reservations due to the age of the student or confidentiality of some information, Parental discretion must be used, but in time youngsters find out many secrets one way or another. Better to learn about family dilemmas in a positive environment.

Every family has interesting episodes in the past since American families come from all over the globe. Share personal stories that give life to the story. When school activities involve family history, parents can talk to the teacher, listen to reports by other students, or give a short talk to the class about your own family.

PARENT GUIDE

Chapter 6
WRITING A HISTORY
OF YOUR FAMILY

Your child's project can be the beginning of a short book. Some books are long and some are short. The family history book can be copyrighted via the web, making your youngster a copyrighted author. In later years the first edition can be lengthened as new information comes to light. Why not help bring this about?

The students have been encouraged to start the project by writing about themselves, and forms are supplied to help with this. A family tree can also be filled out. This lays out contacts to make for vital information. Encourage family, friends and neighbors to offer stories they can tell. The family history story is for the student to write, but you can help much by sharing stories you may not have shared before. Old photos can be copied and thus preserved and shared. They promote recollections also.

Depending on the grade level of the student, the family history may be simply 6-10 pages, but it's a good start.

Chapter 7
THE USE OF COMPUTERS

Most schools now have computers available for students to use. Enormous information is available through their use. Genealogy is not the main object of this project, but nothing is to stop students from looking farther back in time than grandparents. For example, the first person with the name Nava came from northern Spain to Mexico in the 1500's. That may be interesting, but of no practical use. My family history starts with grandparents in practical terms. How far back a student wants to search is a personal choice however.

Most government records are placed into computer memory banks, and the process of expansion continues. This is public information. The Mormon Church has compiled the most extensive memory banks for family surnames. It is part of their faith to record all names possible, whatever the religious faith of the family. On the web Google or AOL are easy to use for access to family name history. Through such tools you might find unknown relatives.

PARENT GUIDE

Chapter 8
USE AND ENJOYMENT OF FAMILY HISTORY

The family history project is a very personal thing. It may be the first time the student's family background has new and deeper meaning. Where a student may want to go in their life may be clearer by looking back into their roots.

Experience shows that family and friends get personally involved in the project when they are asked to take part. Indeed, they may want a copy of the work as a souvenir because they were involved in its production.

Your child will be able to type out his notes and place photos and copies of documents into a short book. It can be added to later as the student grows and the capacity for research develops.

A copy and printing center, like Kinko's, can put the book together at little cost. Gifts of the family history book can be given for Xmas or other holidays. A personal gift like this could not be purchased at a store.

Chapter 9
USING THE FAMILY TREE WORKBOOK

Parents can help the students in **Part Two: Creating the Family Tree Workbook** of this book (see side tabs). By becoming familiar with these materials you are able to help your child more. Adapt or change the charts as you see fit.

Nava family and friends at park gathering, 1957

Parte tres del libro

GUÍA PARA LOS PADRES SOBRE ESCRIBIR LA HISTORÍA DE LA FAMILIA

Capítulo 10
NUESTRA HISTORIA FAMILIAR

Posiblemente sus hijos hayan venido de la escuela con un número de preguntas sobre la familia, pidiendo que Usted les cuente sobre su vida. Podran pedir copias de fotografías viejas o copias de papeles, y que se les lleve a bibliotecas u otros sitios públicos donde se archivan documentos sobre residentes. Todo esto podra ser nuevo, y causar una series de reacciones diversas. Podrá Usted sentirse divertido o molestado. Toda esta actividad resulta de una proyecto en la escuela llamado, " Descubriendo Mi Pasado." Este proyecto se trata de hacer investigaciones sobre la familia y escribir un ensayo sobre esta historia como parte de los trabajos de escuela. Su participación es vital para el exito del proyecto y el desarrollo de sus hijos por medio de comprender mejor su pasado.

Cada familia tiene una historia, desde luego. Los adultos saben muchos detalles de la historia de su familia que los hijos ignoran. Puede pasar mucho tiempo mientras pensamos que mas allá les diremos algunas de estas cosas sobre la familia a los hijos. Entre tanto, los hijos se imaginan el pasado, o se preocupan por lo que no comprenden. A veces crean su propio mundo de fantasías. Tal vez el adulto podrá recordar haber hecho lo mismo en su niñés.

Los jovenes en posesión de una clara comprensión de su historia familiar tendrán mas éxito en su vida. Este éxito comienza con una familiarización de sus raíces y tradiciones familiares. Pudiéramos decir que los jovenes con un conocimiento de su historia conocen mejor "las reglas del juego." Estos jovenes tienen una brújula para orientarlos en la vida. Es mas facil comprender de donde provienen y hacia donde van. No importa que la familia haya tenido episodios dificiles en el pasado, lo mas importante para los jovenes es concocer sus antecedentes y como estos los han afectado.

America es una tierra de inmigrantes porque casi todas las familias vinieron de otro sitio. Solamente los indios vivían aquí cuando los europeos con Colón llegaron en 1492 en busca del oriente. En los EE.UU. casi todo mundo apenas tiene unos docientos años de llegar como inmigrantes desde algún sitio lejano con distintos idiomas y costumbres. Muchos residentes habrán llegado muy recientemente y por lo tanto preservan sus tradiciones y culturas diversas. En todo caso, estas distinctas culturas han enriquecido al país culturalmente. En los EE.UU. las distinctas culturas de sus inmigrantes han creador la mayor riqueza social porque la mezcla de culturas ha creado algo nuevo.

Usted tendrá una oportunidad de enriquezer la vida de sus hijos y sus nietos compartiendo la historia familiar con sus hijos cuando estos vengan de la escuela con preguntas sobre sus raíces. Millones de residentes hoy en día han venido recientemente de lugares sufriendo de condiciones pésimas. Estos residentes nuevos tienen historias fascinantes que contar. Reflexionando sobre ello, muchos detalles de su historia familiar pudieran perderse para siempre por el olvido o la muerte antes de relatarlos o escribirlos. Hay mas peligro de perder la historia familiar en manos de ancianos o amigos de familia grandes. Tan pronto como el proceso de la historia familiar haya comenzado, algo de mucho valor habrá sido creado.

Ambassador Nava's father funeral in 1938 when the future Ambassador was only six.

GUÍA PARA LOS PADRES

Capítulo 11
INTRODUCCION A LA BUSQUEDA DE RAICES FAMILIARES

EL GUIA PARA LOS PADRES facilitará la colaboracíon entre los padres e hijos porque está relacionado capítulo por capítulo con el **Part One: The Student Guide to Creating Family Histories**. En esta forma los padres podrán comprender lo que los estudiantes estan haciendo en la escuela. Utilizando este manual también se facilitará la colaboración con los maestros, lo cual ayuda al estudiante.

Los maestros tienen su propio manual que está relacionado con el de los estudiantes. Con su manual los maestros podrán guiar las actividades de los estudiantes en la escuela. Pero algunos de los trabajos de los estudiantes tendrán que hacerse en casa, con familiares o en otros sitios de la comunidad. Es importante que los padres comprendan la tarea estudiantil de escribir su historia familiar, y que den todo el apoyo posible.

Los tres manuales ofrecen la oportunidad única de que los padres, maestros y los estudiantes tengan la abilidad de colaborar. Esta colaboración es esencial para lograr el éxito. Mas allá, la cooperación de los tres en este proyecto garantizará mayor aprendizaje y desarrollo personal para el estudiante porque aumentará la confianza en sí mismo.

Es convicción de los educadores que cuando los padres colaboran con los maestros y estudiantes estos adquieren un mejor sentido de su papel en la familia, la escuela y la comunidad. Los jovenes formarán un sentido de mas seguridad personal, confianza y lealtad a las instituciones por medio de proyectos como el descubrimiento de sus raíces. Como se relaciona la historia de su familia a la historia de su comunidad, estado y patria se revela por medio de investigar la historia de su propia familia. En efecto, ya que tantas familias norteamericanas son inmigrantes recientes, el conocimiento de la historia familiar aporta para hijos y padres una comprensión mayor de los acontecimientos mundiales que han afectado a la familia. Mayor familiaridad con la geografía, economía y distinctas culturas surge del las actividades relacionadas con buscar la historia familiar.

GUÍA PARA LOS PADRES

Capitulo 12
COMO AYUDAR A LOS HIJOS BUSCAR SUS RAICES FAMILIARES

Mas y mas escuelas tienen computadoras para el uso de los estudiantes porque estas serán indispensables en su vida. En el caso que la escuela tenga computadoras este proyecto está adaptado para utilizar una computadora estilo "Apple." Pero en cualquier caso, el proyecto se puede realizar sin el uso de una computadora. Más abajo, discutiremos como los padres pueden ayudarles a los hijos en cuanto al uso de computadoras en la escuela o en varios sitios de la comunidad. En todo caso, los padres, familiares y amigos de la familia pueden ofrecer mucha información para iniciar los trababjos del estudiante.

Los estudiantes tienen en el Apéndice un formularo que podrán entregar a otros familiares o amigos de la familia con la esperanza de obtener mas información sobre la familia. Este formulario se titula, "Información Contribuida por Familiares y Amigos de La familia." Este formulario podrá rendir muchos datos y una perspectiva distinta sobre la historia familiar. Los padres sabrán hasta que punto ayudar a los hijos en este sentido. No siempre son convenientes las relaciones con algunas personas, desde luego. Si tal fuera el caso, posiblemente los padres querrán dar alguna explicación adecuada a los hijos.

El GUIA PARA LOS PADRES incluye los mismos formularios y diagramas utilizados por los estudiantes. Podrá examinarlos y así estar listo para cuando los hijos vengan de la escuela pidiendo ayuda para colocar los nombres en su sitio, según pertenesca, pidiendo información sobre la historia familiar. También podrá hacer copias de los formularios, enviándolos a parientes lejanos para que ellos colaboren con la información que tengan. Todo esto será parte de un proceso que podrá durar muchos años en el futuro. Los estudiantes ya saben que el proyecto podrá servir como un obsequio para todos los miembros de la familia. Así es que habrá una recompensa para todos los miembros de la gran familia que colaboren, aunque sea por correo.

Algunos pueblos preservan el parentesco usando los appellidos paternales, olvidandose de los maternales. Otras culturas, como la hispana, usan los dos appellidos. Así es que en los EE.UU. mi nombre es simplemente, "Julian Nava." En Latinoamerica, España o las Islas Filipinas mi nombre es "Julian Nava Flores." Flores es el nombre paternal de mi madre. Desde luego, ella tiene un apellido maternal también. Cuando vayan a poner los nombres de familia en los formularios, usen la costumbre social que deseen. Pero recuerden que es mejor que la historia familiar sea lo mas completa posible.

El manual da indicaciones de posible fuentes de información, tales como dependencias gubernamentales igual que grupos privados que colectan datos sobre historia familiar. Algunos grupos reunen datos geneológicos, eso es decir quien parió a quién. Sin embargo, historia familiar es mucho mas que simple geneología porque trata de como vivieron los mucho antepasados y las condiciones de su época.

Muchas otras actividades interesantes pueden resultar si la clase entera embarca en este proyecto. Los estudiantes podrán dar breves presentaciones sobre la historia de su familia ante la clase, y algunos padres podrán platicarle a la clase sobre la familia y sus aventuras. Algunos padres habrán tenido experiencias casi de novela o para hacer una película. Podra ser muy interesante comparar la vida de distintas familias. Usted y sus hijos podrán llegar a ser expertos en su historia familiar debido a este proyecto escolar.

Este proyecto podrá ofrecer la primera ocasión para que los tres-- padres, hijos y maestros--colaboren en la educación del estudiante. Si fuera así, descubrirán el gusto de tomar parte activa en la educación de sus hijos. Este manual podrá acercar miembros de la familia.

Capítulo 13
COMO BUSCAR FUENTES DE INFORMACION SOBRE LA HISTORIA FAMILIAR

Las fuentes de información mas utiles para los estudiantes serán los padres, tutores, parientes o amigos de la familia. Los maestros animarán a los estudiantes que escriban a familiares u otras personas que sepan de la familia. Los padres podrán ayudar dando nombres y señas de personas indicadas. La escritura de cartas a conocidos podrá ser parte de las prácticas literarias en la clase, y a la vez establecer lazos más íntimos entre diversos miembros de la gran familia. En el caso que intervenga otro idioma entre las generaciones, este proyecto servirá para promover bilinguismo también. Esta habilidad bilingue será de mucho valor en la vida del estudiante.

Varias dependencias de gobierno archivan datos sobre familias y esta información se ofrece al público gratis en persona o por carta. Cada pueblo, ciudad, municipio, estado, igual que las dependencias federales mantienen archivos. Si la familia vino al país recientemente, habrá necesidad de comunicarse con las dependencias de otro gobierno. Esto complica la tarea, pero todo gobierno mantiene archivos sobre sus residentes y ciudadanos. Por otro lado, iglesias o grupos religiosos también mantienen archivos por mucho tiempo, y son buenas fuentes de información. Algunos grupos, como los Mormones, colectan y mantienen archivos excelentes sobre nombres y familias, con fechas de vida y parentesco. Estos archivos son generales, e incluyen personas que no sean mormones. Les da igual, y ofrecen colaborar con cualquier persona sin obligación religiosa. Estos archivos mormones estan registrados por computadora, y por lo tanto son muy acsesibles.

Aquí tienen una lista de fuentes de información, comenzando con las más fáciles, hasta llegar a las más difíciles. Probablemente sus hijos van a necesitar ayuda para contactar las fuentes que están más lejos de donde viven o las que están en otro país. Los padres podrán ayudarles con esta parte de la tarea.

Su familia (pueden hablarles o escribirles a ellos)

- ✔ padres,
- ✔ hermanos y hermanas
- ✔ abuelos,
- ✔ tíos y tías,
- ✔ primos

ARCHIVOS DE IGLESIA

Contratos de matrimonio, registro de bautismos y muertes que se preservan por muchos años, (a veces siglos).

Archivos de familias en la memoria de las computadoras están disponibles al público.

Archivos de la Iglesia Mormona

Hay archivos sobre nombres y familias abiertos a todo mundo en Salt Lake City, Utah y por la web.

Archivos de gobierno local

Registros de nacimiento, matrimonio, impuestos, licencia de operar negocios etc., se preservan y están abiertos al público.

Archivos del estado

Varias licencias que existen en registros, tales como las de conducir coches, algunos negocios, ciertas profesiones. Ayuda social al individuo (préstamos del estado al individuo, becas, servicios médicos, seguro social Etc)

Archivos del gobierno nacional

(Los Archivos Nacionales contienen información de los últimos 200 años)

✔ archivos de servicio militar refieren a familias y no solamente al individuo

✔ Archivos de aduanas registran toda persona que cruza la frontera

✔ Los archivos del Seguro Social existen que desde 1930

✔ Mucha de la información que hay en los Archivos Nacional después de 1819, la pueden obtener en copias fotostáticas

GUÍA PARA LOS PADRES

porque se encuentran en las bibliotecas de los estados. La maestra de escuela o la biblioteca local podrá ayudarle establecer contacto con estas dependencias porque es parte de su trababjo. Como pueden ver, hay mucha ayuda a la mano. Depende del tiempo en el pasado que quieran investigar y con cuanto detalle.

Los hijos e incluso los padres podrán estar haciendo estas investigaciones por la primera vez, y podrá ser extraño al principio. Asi es que calquier colaboración entre los padres e hijos promoverá un sentido de equipo y amistad que rendirá frutos en el futuro para toda la familia.

Julian Nava, his sister Rosemaria, and her son Steven Herzig Nava at his graduation from the U.S. Airforce Academy

Capitulo 14
TRABAJANDO CON LA ESCUELA

Sus hijos trabajaran con varios grupos en la escuela, tales con los maestros, los compañeros de clase, la biblioteca Etc. Para algunos estudiantes, este tipo de trato con personas y grupos será nuevo y podrá causar cierto nerviosismo. La colaboración de los padres es un elemento muy importante para los hijos porque cuando los padres apoyen a los hijos y tomen parte en algunas de las actividades de escuela relacionadas con el proyecto esto dará mucho ánimo a los hijos.

Suele ser el caso con estudiantes que hablan español comunmente en la casa desde la ninez tengan dificultad con el ingles en escuela. Esta dificultad puede ser gran problema para los estudiantes por una serie de razones. Los maestros no siempre hablan español, y no tienen mucho tiempo para dar instrucción en dos idiomas sin perjudicar la agenda de estudios. Otros estudiantes a veces se burlan del que no habla Inglés correctamente. Desde luego, los estudiantes en estos casos pierden terreno y se quedan atrás de los demás compañeros de clase. Debido a un sentido de desesperación, muchos estudiantes hispanos se fugan de la escuela.

Cuando los padres participen con este proyecto les darán a los hijos un gran empuje. El estudiante entonces se sentirá respaldado por su familia. El éxito del estudiante en este proyecto le dará la confianza para superar los desafíos que cualquier estudiante de origen inmigrante confronta. Todos los otros grupos de inmigrantes de Europa o Asia pasan por la mismas experiencias, y el papel de los padres llega a ser un factor primordial en el éxito de los hijos en la escuela. No importa que la ayuda a los hijos sea en español (o chino), lo importante es que los padres participen en tales proyectos con los hijos.

View of the ruins of the Nava family home in Mexico after Mexican Revolution (through archway)

Capítulo 15
COMO ESCRIBIR LA HISTORIA FAMILIAR

GUÍA PARA LOS PADRES

EN COLABORACION CON LOS HIJOS

No cabe duda que cada familia tiene episodios interesantes en su historia. Piensen sobre estos para cuando sus hijos les hagan preguntas. Hagan notas sobre temas interesantes. Recuerden que lo familiar para los padres podrá ser una gran revelación para los hijos. Habrá archivos de la familia? Cartas, fotos o documentos viejos estarán guardados por allí. Estos servirán para estimular la memoria de los padres.

En el caso que algunos documentos o fotos estén en mala condición, este proyecto servirá como pretexto para hacer copias, y así asegurar la preservación de ellos para el futuro. Aún la música vieja provoca la memoria de aventuras, romances y eventos importantes Pláticas con amigos viejos podrá rendir a gran cantidad de información también.

Los padres representan una mina de oro sobre el pasado que puede enriquecer a los hijos, y los otros alumnos también. Habrá padres que deseen dar una plática a la clase sobre algún episodio de la historia familiar. No importa que sea en español, al contrario, es un orgullo hablar un idioma tan bello como el español. Los hijos nuestros podrán traducir para la clase en tal caso. Que lindo sería que en una ocasión unos padres cuenten algo de la historia familiar a la clase en chino, ruso o español, y no solamente en inglés.

La colaboración de los padres en este simple proyecto puede rendir muchos beneficios, como hemos visto. Cuando los hijos vean esta forma de testamento por parte de sus padres, sentirán un orgullo por sus raîces que les ayudará superar cualquier obstaculo en su vida.

Es posible que sus hijos traten de escribir un libro pequeño sobre la familia, basándose en la información que obtengan de usted y las otras fuentes de información. Los maestros les ayudarán con esta tarea, según el nivel escolar. En tal caso los padres tendrán una gran oportunidad de colaborar en esta obra literaria. Cualquier nivel de trabajo hecho por su hijo tendrá la gracia de ser su obra sobre un tema de gran importancia para él. En los años futuros, esta obra tendra aún mas valor sentimental para no solamente los padres, sino para los hijos mismos y los nietos también.

Capitulo 16
EL USO DE COMPUTADORAS PARA INVESTIGAR EL PASADO

Aunque la escuela de nuestros hijos no tenga una computadora para uso de los estudiantes es posible hacer uso de las computadoras en manos de varios grupos en la comunidad. Por lo tanto es bueno que los padres sepan algo de computadoras y como hacer uso de los servicios que en casi todos los casos son gratis.

Varios grupos en los Estados Unidos y Europa están haciendo grandes listas de nombres de individuos, familias y fechas de actos familiares importantes, para archivarlos en las memorias de las computadoras. Estas memorias, se conocen con el nombre de "bancos de información o de datos." Las computadoras con estos bancos de información se conectan con las escuelas, oficinas, casa y cualquier lugar, a través de las líneas telefónicas por medio de un pequeño aparato electrónico llamado un "modem," que sirve de traductor entre las dos computadoras.

GUÍA PARA LOS PADRES

En el caso que la escuela tenga computadora, la información sobre la familia se puede grabar dentro de un "disco" pequeño. El estudiante puede llevárselo a casa, lo cual hace posible que el estudiante conecte con otras computadoras en la comunidad que contienen colecciones muy grandes de nombres de otras familias. Algunas de estas colecciones contienen los nombres de millones de nombres por todo el mundo desde hace dos o mas siglos. La información en estas colecciones se comparte gratis, casi siempre.

Como hemos observado antes, la historia familiar es mucho más amplia que la geneología simple, porque ésta únicamente estudia los parentescos con otras personas. En cambio la historia familiar,"su historia familiar," abarca la vida de sus padres, abuelos y hasta los más viejos antepasados, lo que hicieron y cómo vivieron en épocas pasadas. Es por eso que pueden aprender mucho sobre las condiciones físicas, sociales e inclusive hasta económicas de sus antepasados. Sin embargo, el inicio de la historia de su familia es la recolección de nombres y fechas de sus parientes más cercanos.

Parece raro, pero en vista de esta revolución de intercambio de información, muchas personas han encontrado a miembros de su familia que estaban perdidos y eran desconocidos. También, verán que muchos individuos descienden de personajes importantes de la historia, aunque el conocimiento de la relación se haya perdido. Por eso son muy importantes los "bancos de información" de computadoras, porque de alguna forma les pueden ayudar a descubrir el pasado desconocido.

Capitulo 17
COMO PUEDEN UTILIZAR SU HISTORIA FAMILILAR

La historia de su familia es para el uso personal y para los archivos futuros de la familia. Esta historia le dará al estudiente un conocimiento firme de quien es y de donde viene. Desde luego, al comenzar la labor de escribir su historia familiar, comenzara un proyecto que durará mas tiempo de lo que se le dedica en la escuela este año. Con este inicio toda la familia podrá seguir la pista de la historia familiar por su cuenta. Mucha mas información quedará por descubrir después de estos primeros esfuerzos. Después, cada generación podrá añadir lo suyo.

Encontrarán que los parientes con los cuales hayan hablado, tendrán mucha curiosidad sobre sus revelaciones. Probablemente, ustedes habrán dedicado más tiempo a este trabajo sobre su familia que cualquier otro brazo de la familia. Por lo tanto, usted y sus hijos tendrán en sus manos un regalo muy especial para sus amados. Podrán, por ejemplo, hacer copias de su historia y regalarlas como obsequio para cumple años, Navidades u otras ocasiones. Cuando hayan recogido información, cuentos o fotografías de sus parientes y antepasados, será mucho mas valioso que una simple lista de nombres (geneología). Será esta historia, un archivo único, rico e interesante.

Posiblemente descubrirán un gran heroe en el pasado de la familia, un gran pintor, un inventor o un bandido! No es posible saber ahora lo que puedan descubrir y compartir. Los padres podrán ayudar a los hijos con las sorpresas que pudieran resultar.

Con los medios a la mano hoy es possible hacer copias de la historia familiar y dar estas como obsequios para Navidad u otra occasion especial. Este obsequio personal no fuera possible comprar.

Nava, Hernandez, Munatones, Wrightson, Goodlaw. Guerra
family surnames at family wedding

Julian and Ruth Nava in Los Angeles in 1934

Part Four of the Book
The Teachers
Guide To Creating
Family Histories

Preface To The Teachers Handbook

A project like researching and writing one's family history may not have a place in the ordinary school curriculum. Until it does have a place in the curriculum, the teacher can find a place and means to engage in this activity. The family history project has broad value. In writing a family history the student becomes an active participant in research, interviewing, note taking and writing. This project is suitable for Middle School, High School or even college. Student goals and classroom expectations will vary according to grade level.

The project may be assigned or be voluntary. Extra credit may be given for such independent study. To avoid interrupting a mandated weekly schedule, it can work if some time on Fridays is dedicated to family history class work. This gives students the weekend to do research. Oral reports or class discussion next Friday is workable. Teachers may use wide latitude in ways to promote the project activity and involve parents.

The family history project is based on the conviction

TEACHER GUIDE

that stronger bonds with one's family are vital in the face of social change and questionable influences that bear on young people today.

The Teachers Handbook will serve to help teachers guide students in the search for their family history. This family history project is suitable for various grades in public schools, and for adults as well. Indeed, after starting the project in one grade, students can supplement the project in later classes at a higher level of research skill development. Thus, the initial work on the family history project might progress as the student grows and develops. In the event the teacher assigns the project to the entire class, the handbooks contain suggestions about activities that would involve the entire class as a group. Handbooks for parents in English and Spanish can help involve the entire family in family history activities currently underway in the school. Parental involvement with their students in school activities is all to the good.

The teacher will find specific suggestions and models for classroom activities that relate the search for family history to most academic areas. Teachers may shape these activities to grade level or ability level. In the event that some students cannot communicate well in English, they could develop their family history project in their dominant language. This flexibility would provide a valuable outlet for abilities that are not restricted by a student's or family limitations in English. The translating of a family history project can be a valuable bridge to the acquisition of English.

Student competence can be increased in subjects like economics, geography, history, writing and speaking by tailoring the activities outlined in this handbook. Of course, the personal relevance of the family history will increase the interest of the pupil in all these subjects, with only modest guidance by the teacher. Students will see how their family history involves all subject areas, which are commonly studied in isolation and in an impersonal manner.

Nava with Tibetan girls atop Potola Palace in Lhasa, Tibet

TEACHER GUIDE

Chapter 1
YOUR FAMILY HISTORY

Activities before the reading of **Part One: The Student Guide to Creating Family Histories,** Chapter 1 can arouse student interest. You may choose to tell about your family to encourage students to look into their own family.

Sample teacher questions to the class.

- ✔ How many brothers and sisters have you?

- ✔ How many relatives do you have? What are their names?

- ✔ How many have grandparents are still living?

- ✔ Illicit oral remarks to the class about parents, such as:

- ✔ Where were they each born?

- ✔ How they meet each other?

- ✔ An interesting or exciting event in their lives

- ✔ Parental goals and aspirations for you

✔ Identify geographic location of family origins.

Place pins on a map to illustrate global origins of students.

STUDENTS MAY READ CHAPTER I OF THE STUDENT HANDBOOK SILENTLY IN CLASS OR AT HOME

Possible class activity after reading **Part One: The Student Guide to Creating Family Histories**, Chapter 1

- Promote class discussion about how information or records are stored. How have computers added to information found in books, video, films, photos, Etc. What other ways are there to store data?

For developing some basic skills, discuss terms such as these:

Define the following words, relating them to everyday life.

1. ancestor

2. generation

3. traditions

4. computer

5. memory capacity

6. identify other terms appropriate to grade level or class work

Making up a family tree – Using the charts in **Part Two: Creating the Family Tree Workbook,** students list relatives and write their names on the branches of a chart. Our goal is to trace family history back to grandparents only. With this modest start students may choose to search back farther on their own.

****

A Note for the Teacher. Teachers should make sure that all students understand the basics of what computers are and what they can do. The following student activities may be helpful in this regard.

Help students to practice using a computer in school. If the school does not have a computer for students to use, students may go to a computer store with parents and get acquainted with computers. Perhaps they can visit a friend who has a computer. Help students to record family information on the computer and get a printout of the information. Students will now be acquainted with using a computer in a new manner.

Encourage students to record parent's recollections on cassette tape when available. Students that do not have a cassette recorder can write down what they learn, promoting writing skills. Students may ask parents for family pictures. Old pictures, often just stored away, can make a new family treasure when incorporated into a family history.

CHAPTER 2
AN INTRODUCTION TO THE SEARCH FOR FAMILY ROOTS

SAMPLE QUESTIONS FOR THE TEACHER TO POSE FOR DISCUSSION

- ✔ How far back into time can you remember?
- ✔ Can you remember before you were born?
- ✔ Why do we sometimes forget memories and remember others?
- ✔ What can we do to help remember better?
- ✔ How are we similar to our current relatives?
- ✔ How are we affected by nutrition, climate and so forth?

TEACHER GUIDE

STUDENTS READ CHAPTER 2 OF THE STUDENT HANDBOOK

Teacher may ask students to list the characteristics of the family member they most resemble, or whom they "take after" in personality and interests. Students may save the description for compiling their family history album.

Sample activities: students may or use the following terms in sentences:

1. origins (personal, family, racial, cultural Etc.}

2. time zones

3. descendants

4. characteristics

5. future

6. others terms appropriate to the class

CHAPTER 3
HOW TO USE THIS HANDBOOK

QUESTIONS TO PROMOTE UNDERSTANDING.

Ask students:

1. Whether they have a bank account?

2. What things do people do at a bank (e.g. put in money, take out money, etc)?

3 Can students name banks that do not deal with money (e.g. blood banks, computer banks, etc.)?

Teacher: Now that we know there are computer banks available to us, students read Chapter 3 to find out how to use computer information to research family history and combine that ability with this manual.

STUDENTS READ CHAPTER 3 SILENTLY OR AT HOME

TEACHER GUIDE

Teacher: Did you find out how to get information about your family past and present? How can computers help? Where else can you go for information about your family? How valuable are human sources?

CLASS ACTIVITIES

1. Students obtain a blank of the world and color in the areas their parents and grandparents came from, and if possible great grandparents.

2. Students make a list of countries and continents represented by ancestors of all class members. A large map on the wall drives home global representation of the student body.

CHAPTER 4
FINDING SOURCES OF INFORMATION FOR THE FAMILY HISTORY

TEACHER POSES MOTIVATIONAL QUESTIONS.

Which TV detective shows do you watch?

Do you have a favorite show?

Have you ever wanted to be a detective?

What does a detective do?

STUDENTS READ CHAPTER 4.

Teacher may ask:

1. What sources of information did you learn about?

2. What are the ways you can contact these people and

places (letters, telephone, visits in person etc.)

3. Which people would be easiest for you to contact?

SKILL DEVELOPMENT.

Students discuss the following questions:

1. Which religious groups keep the accurate records on family history?

2. How can your teacher or librarian help you with the family history?

3. How do governments help to keep family records?

President Jimmy Carter (on the right) with Cyrus Vance, Secretary of State and U.S. Ambassador to Mexico Julian Nava in 1979

CHAPTER 5
WORKING WITH
THE SCHOOL

TEACHER PROMOTES DISCUSSIONS ON THE FOLLOWING SUBJECTS:

1. What else does the school do for you besides teach?

2. Which resources do you think are available at your school for compiling your family history?

IMPLEMENTATION OF THE LESSON:

Students read Chapter 5 of the Student Guide.

Students list school resources.

Students discuss how school resources can help write one's family history.

"HANDS ON" ACTIVITIES.

1. Students may choose to discuss their family history

TEACHER GUIDE

project with neighbors.

2. Students may select an interesting episode of their family history and write a short essay about this, illustrating the essay with photographs. This simple exercise can build confidence for writing a family history later.

3. Some more out-going students may choose to make an oral presentation to the class about an episode in their family history.

Munatones/Nava castle in Northern Spain

CHAPTER 6
WRITING A
FAMILY HISTORY

STUDENTS READ CHAPTER 6

Teacher asks:

1. Have you found any surprises in your family history so far?

2. What can you do if your information is incomplete?

3. Ask students to list the foreign languages their ancestors spoke. How many languages did ancestors of the class speak?

HELPING STUDENTS WRITE A BOOK ABOUT THEIR FAMILY HISTORY

For some students writing a short book about their family history will be an amazing undertaking. Yet, the project is quite within the realm of possibility when the teacher takes stock of the grade level and ability of the students. Granted, some students would be hard-pressed to put together only five pages of materials, while others could write a "term paper."

At the end of Chapter 6 in the Student Manual we find some suggestions for students regarding writing a short book on their family history. The Student Manual contains different charts or questionnaires for interviews. Some of these forms could be gathered from numerous family members or family friends. By simply joining together these materials with some prefatory and concluding remarks, as well as photos and documents, we could have the start of a book.

You can offer to help students start a short book about their family history. This offer can help put students at ease. Point out that every book (or essay) for example, has a beginning, middle and an end. Describe the features of each of the three parts. Writing a book is that simple

A simple manila folder can bind the written work. Some students may want to include illustrations, or copies of photos or documents about themselves or the family. This work is only a beginning effort, which students can add to as part of schoolwork in another class or later in life. A standard paper size is advisable because it facilitates making copies of the work. Copy-making centers like Kinko's can help make a family history into a very attractive personal gift for friends and family.

CHAPTER 7
USING COMPUTER DATA BANKS TO SEARCH FAR BACK INTO TIME

TEACHER GUIDE

MOTIVATIONAL QUESTIONS FOR STUDENTS TO DISCUSS:

1. What is history? How can history be recorded?

2. Why can it be important to keep track of our past?

3. How can we use the information from the past to help us now?

IMPLEMENTATION OF THE LESSON:

STUDENTS READ **Part One: Student Guide,** Chapter 7 in class or at home

SKILL DEVELOPMENT:

Teacher----- To help students reach a workable level of computer skills, demonstrate to them some of the computer search engines available. Try www.Ancestry.com in the classroom, if available.

"HANDS ON" ACTIVITIES:

If possible students visit the nearest Mormon computer bank of family history. Note that assistance is non-religious. Parents may take students there.

Through simple library research students can find out about the people who lived thousands of years ago in the same regions that their ancestors came from. Students can make a chart and/or write a story about these ancestors.

Julian Nava viewing the ruins of family home in Salitral destroyed in 1915 during the Mexican Revolution

CHAPTER 8
HOW TO USE YOUR FAMILY HISTORY

SAMPLE QUESTIONSFOR CLASS DISCUSSON:

Teacher asks: Suppose you write an essay on your family history.

Who can use your family history?

How could it be used?

Teacher---- Now that we have speculated about the use for the family history, read Chapter 8 to find out how it could be used.

TEACHER GUIDE

STUDENTS READ CHAPTER 8

Teacher: How many uses for the family history did you find?

Now that you understand why you are undertaking this project, how can it have special meaning to you?

SKILL DEVELOPMENT:

Students recite how their family members might react when they receive the family history as a gift. The more outspoken students may inspire others to speak up. The teacher may fictionalize their own story to make it more interesting for students.

"HANDS ON" ACTIVITIES

Students record the birthdays of all living relatives. This data will be handy for future use.

Most English, Germanic, French and Hispanic families have a family insignia or crest. A computer search engine will reveal illustrated heraldic sources in English and Spanish.

After identifying their family crest, students may draw theirs or put a photocopy in the essay. Identifying one's paternal and maternal family crests will supply a new link to the ancient past. How crests got started is fascinating. Again, for our purposes this handbook seeks to help trace family history back to grandparents.

Students may ask parents to have a family meeting to discuss how relatives may help with the family history project.

CHAPTER 9
USING THE FAMILY TREE WORKBOOK

Teacher reviews the charts in **Part Two: Creating the Family Tree Workbook** of this book (see side tabs) to help students with their use. It will be helpful if each chart is on a separate page for work.

The first chart deals with basic data about the student/ author.

TEACHER GUIDE

CHAPTER 10
SUGGESTED CULMINATION ACTIVITIES

1. Have the children ask their parents to come to the classroom and tell about an interesting or exciting event in the family's history.

2. Ask students to bring videos or films of their family. Students could show five to ten minutes of film in his or her individual presentation.

3. Have a field trip to a computer bank so that children can experiment with the machines firsthand. A public library may serve much the same end.

4. Prepare a display of family history projects and invite parents and colleagues to view the work.

5. Invite a speaker from a local historical society or genealogy group to speak to the class.

6. Contact local or community-oriented newspapers to give recognition to student family history projects. Some

local business may want to sponsor printing class family projects.

7. Local television stations may want to highlight the project or aspects of the rich cultural heritage embodied in the students of your school as part of an effort to promote civic pride

8. Some students may want to copyright their work. This can be done by use of the Internet. The students could thus become copyrighted authors. Why not?

Colonel Andy Hernandez/Nava and cousin Steven Herzig/ Nava at his Airforce Academy graduation

TEACHER GUIDE

Part Five of the Book
THE TOP 350
HISPANIC SURNAMES
IN THE UNITED STATES

INTRODUCTION

We all have a last name - and it is very key component to tracing our ancestry. Some people have been able to trace their ancestry back over 600 years in large part because of our last names, also known as surnames. In the United States there are 151,671 last names that 100 people or more share.

Our research found that 7,766, or 5.1% of the universe mentioned above are Hispanic surnames. 64% of all Hispanics in the USA use the top 350 of those names. In this section we offer details of those top 350 names.

The rankings are for both how Hispanic surnames rank and where these individual surnames fall within all the surnames in the United States (Overall). The second line of the data shows where the individuals classified themselves. While the vast majorities of these individuals see themselves as Hispanic, some are non-Hispanic whites, African Americans, American Indians, and Asian American. People identifying with two races make up any additional percentages to make 100%. All the data presented here is from the 2000 Census. In future editions we will have information from the 2010 Census as it becomes available.

This section of the book is designed for children and adults to explore and learn more about both their name - and that of friends and family. *Have fun exploring.*

TOP 350 HISPANIC SURNAMES

GARCIA **Ranking:** 1 *Hispanic* 8 *Overall* USA Total People: **858,289**
90.8% Hispanic **6.2%** White **0.5%**Black **0.6%** Am. Indian **1.4%** Asian Pac.Is.

RODRIGUEZ **Ranking:** 2 *Hispanic* 9 *Overall* USA Total People: **804,240**
92.7% Hispanic **5.5%** White **0.5%**Black **0.2%** Am. Indian **0.6%** Asian Pac.Is.

MARTINEZ **Ranking:** 3 *Hispanic* 11 *Overall* USA Total People: **775,072**
91.7% Hispanic **6.0%** White **0.5%**Black **0.6%** Am. Indian **0.6%** Asian Pac.Is.

HERNANDEZ **Ranking:** 4 *Hispanic* 15 *Overall* USA Total People: **706,372**
93.8% Hispanic **4.6%** White **0.4%**Black **0.3%** Am. Indian **0.7%** Asian Pac.Is.

LOPEZ **Ranking:** 5 *Hispanic* 21 *Overall* USA Total People: **621,536**
91.5% Hispanic **5.9%** White **0.6%**Black **0.5%** Am. Indian **1.0%** Asian Pac.Is.

GONZALEZ **Ranking:** 6 *Hispanic* 23 *Overall* USA Total People: **597,718**
94.0% Hispanic **4.8%** White **0.4%**Black **0.2%** Am. Indian **0.4%** Asian Pac.Is.

PEREZ **Ranking:** 7 *Hispanic* 29 *Overall* USA Total People: **488,521**
91.7% Hispanic **6.0%** White **0.5%**Black **0.3%** Am. Indian **1.2%** Asian Pac.Is.

SANCHEZ **Ranking:** 8 *Hispanic* 33 *Overall* USA Total People: **441,242**
91.8% Hispanic **5.8%** White **0.5%**Black **0.5%** Am. Indian **1.0%** Asian Pac.Is.

RAMIREZ **Ranking:** 9 *Hispanic* 42 *Overall* USA Total People: **388,987**
93.7% Hispanic **4.4%** White **0.3%**Black **0.3%** Am. Indian **1.0%** Asian Pac.Is.

TORRES **Ranking:** 10 *Hispanic* 50 *Overall* USA Total People: **325,169**
91.2% Hispanic **6.1%** White **0.6%**Black **0.3%** Am. Indian **1.4%** Asian Pac.Is.

FLORES **Ranking:** 11 *Hispanic* 55 *Overall* USA Total People: **312,615**
90.8% Hispanic **5.6%** White **0.5%**Black **0.4%** Am. Indian **2.2%** Asian Pac.Is.

RIVERA **Ranking:** 12 *Hispanic* 59 *Overall* USA Total People: **299,463**
90.2% Hispanic **5.9%** White **1.1%**Black **0.2%** Am. Indian **2.1%** Asian Pac.Is.

GOMEZ **Ranking:** 13 *Hispanic* 68 *Overall* USA Total People: **263,590**
91.2% Hispanic **6.1%** White **0.8%**Black **0.3%** Am. Indian **1.0%** Asian Pac.Is.

DIAZ **Ranking:** 14 *Hispanic* 73 *Overall* USA Total People: **251,772**
91.2% Hispanic **6.2%** White **0.7%**Black **0.2%** Am. Indian **1.2%** Asian Pac.Is.

REYES **Ranking:** 15 *Hispanic* 81 *Overall* USA Total People: **232,511**
86.9% Hispanic **5.3%** White **0.8%**Black **0.3%** Am. Indian **6.0%** Asian Pac.Is.

CRUZ **Ranking:** 16 *Hispanic* 82 *Overall* USA Total People: **231,065**
86.2% Hispanic **6.0%** White **0.8%**Black **0.4%** Am. Indian **5.6%** Asian Pac.Is.

MORALES **Ranking:** 17 *Hispanic* 90 *Overall* USA Total People: **217,642**
91.9% Hispanic **5.6%** White **0.6%**Black **0.3%** Am. Indian **1.2%** Asian Pac.Is.

ORTIZ **Ranking:** 18 *Hispanic* 94 *Overall* USA Total People: **214,683**
92.4% Hispanic **5.4%** White **0.6%**Black **0.5%** Am. Indian **0.7%** Asian Pac.Is.

GUTIERREZ   Ranking: **19** *Hispanic*   **96** *Overall*   USA Total People: **212,905**
92.4% Hispanic   **5.2%** White   **0.3%** Black   **0.3%** Am. Indian   **1.4%** Asian Pac. Is.

GONZALES   Ranking: **20** *Hispanic*   **110** *Overall*   USA Total People: **193,934**
84.4% Hispanic   **10.0%** White   **0.9%** Black   **0.8%** Am. Indian   **3.1%** Asian Pac. Is.

RAMOS   Ranking: **21** *Hispanic*   **112** *Overall*   USA Total People: **193,096**
85.4% Hispanic   **7.2%** White   **0.9%** Black   **0.3%** Am. Indian   **5.0%** Asian Pac. Is.

CHAVEZ   Ranking: **22** *Hispanic*   **118** *Overall*   USA Total People: **185,865**
92.0% Hispanic   **5.7%** White   **0.2%** Black   **1.2%** Am. Indian   **0.6%** Asian Pac. Is.

RUIZ   Ranking: **23** *Hispanic*   **129** *Overall*   USA Total People: **175,429**
91.7% Hispanic   **6.1%** White   **0.5%** Black   **0.3%** Am. Indian   **1.0%** Asian Pac. Is.

ALVAREZ   Ranking: **24** *Hispanic*   **132** *Overall*   USA Total People: **168,817**
90.7% Hispanic   **6.6%** White   **0.6%** Black   **0.5%** Am. Indian   **1.2%** Asian Pac. Is.

MENDOZA   Ranking: **25** *Hispanic*   **134** *Overall*   USA Total People: **168,567**
88.6% Hispanic   **4.9%** White   **0.4%** Black   **0.3%** Am. Indian   **5.2%** Asian Pac. Is.

CASTILLO   Ranking: **26** *Hispanic*   **135** *Overall*   USA Total People: **165,473**
88.9% Hispanic   **5.6%** White   **0.8%** Black   **0.8%** Am. Indian   **3.3%** Asian Pac. Is.

VASQUEZ   Ranking: **27** *Hispanic*   **143** *Overall*   USA Total People: **159,989**
92.5% Hispanic   **5.5%** White   **0.5%** Black   **0.4%** Am. Indian   **0.7%** Asian Pac. Is.

JIMENEZ   Ranking: **28** *Hispanic*   **147** *Overall*   USA Total People: **157,475**
93.0% Hispanic   **4.5%** White   **0.3%** Black   **0.3%** Am. Indian   **1.5%** Asian Pac. Is.

ROMERO   Ranking: **29** *Hispanic*   **154** *Overall*   USA Total People: **153,772**
86.1% Hispanic   **10.4%** White   **0.5%** Black   **1.0%** Am. Indian   **1.3%** Asian Pac. Is.

MORENO   Ranking: **30** *Hispanic*   **170** *Overall*   USA Total People: **146,088**
91.0% Hispanic   **7.1%** White   **0.4%** Black   **0.5%** Am. Indian   **0.6%** Asian Pac. Is.

HERRERA   Ranking: **31** *Hispanic*   **175** *Overall*   USA Total People: **140,786**
91.9% Hispanic   **5.6%** White   **0.4%** Black   **0.7%** Am. Indian   **1.0%** Asian Pac. Is.

MEDINA   Ranking: **32** *Hispanic*   **176** *Overall*   USA Total People: **139,353**
90.1% Hispanic   **6.4%** White   **0.5%** Black   **0.4%** Am. Indian   **2.0%** Asian Pac. Is.

FERNANDEZ   Ranking: **33** *Hispanic*   **178** *Overall*   USA Total People: **139,302**
80.7% Hispanic   **11.4%** White   **1.3%** Black   **0.2%** Am. Indian   **5.2%** Asian Pac. Is.

CASTRO   Ranking: **34** *Hispanic*   **194** *Overall*   USA Total People: **133,254**
85.5% Hispanic   **8.7%** White   **0.7%** Black   **0.3%** Am. Indian   **3.8%** Asian Pac. Is.

AGUILAR   Ranking: **35** *Hispanic*   **213** *Overall*   USA Total People: **126,399**
92.2% Hispanic   **4.7%** White   **0.2%** Black   **0.7%** Am. Indian   **1.7%** Asian Pac. Is.

SILVA   Ranking: **36** *Hispanic*   **214** *Overall*   USA Total People: **126,164**
58.2% Hispanic   **33.7%** White   **1.2%** Black   **0.4%** Am. Indian   **1.8%** Asian Pac. Is.

TOP 350 HISPANIC SURNAMES

GARZA Ranking: 37 *Hispanic* 220 *Overall* USA Total People: **124,130**
92.5% Hispanic **6.6%** White **0.2%** Black **0.3%** Am. Indian **0.2%** Asian Pac.Is.

VARGAS Ranking: 38 *Hispanic* 221 *Overall* USA Total People: **123,952**
91.8% Hispanic **6.2%** White **0.4%** Black **0.2%** Am. Indian **0.8%** Asian Pac.Is.

GUZMAN Ranking: 39 *Hispanic* 230 *Overall* USA Total People: **118,390**
92.7% Hispanic **4.7%** White **0.5%** Black **0.2%** Am. Indian **1.4%** Asian Pac.Is.

MUNOZ Ranking: 40 *Hispanic* 232 *Overall* USA Total People: **117,774**
92.6% Hispanic **5.5%** White **0.3%** Black **0.3%** Am. Indian **0.9%** Asian Pac.Is.

SALAZAR Ranking: 41 *Hispanic* 240 *Overall* USA Total People: **113,468**
90.9% Hispanic **6.1%** White **0.3%** Black **0.6%** Am. Indian **1.6%** Asian Pac.Is.

MENDEZ Ranking: 42 *Hispanic* 242 *Overall* USA Total People: **112,736**
92.6% Hispanic **5.3%** White **0.8%** Black **0.4%** Am. Indian **0.5%** Asian Pac.Is.

SOTO Ranking: 43 *Hispanic* 257 *Overall* USA Total People: **106,631**
92.3% Hispanic **5.9%** White **0.6%** Black **0.3%** Am. Indian **0.5%** Asian Pac.Is.

SANTOS Ranking: 44 *Hispanic* 279 *Overall* USA Total People: **98,993**
58.3% Hispanic **21.9%** White **1.8%** Black **0.3%** Am. Indian **13.2%** Asian Pac.Is.

DELGADO Ranking: 45 *Hispanic* 282 *Overall* USA Total People: **98,675**
91.3% Hispanic **6.5%** White **0.7%** Black **0.2%** Am. Indian **0.7%** Asian Pac.Is.

VALDEZ Ranking: 46 *Hispanic* 283 *Overall* USA Total People: **98,610**
87.8% Hispanic **6.8%** White **0.5%** Black **0.7%** Am. Indian **3.4%** Asian Pac.Is.

PENA Ranking: 47 *Hispanic* 284 *Overall* USA Total People: **98,345**
91.6% Hispanic **5.9%** White **0.5%** Black **0.4%** Am. Indian **1.1%** Asian Pac.Is.

RIOS Ranking: 48 *Hispanic* 285 *Overall* USA Total People: **96,569**
93.0% Hispanic **5.3%** White **0.5%** Black **0.4%** Am. Indian **0.4%** Asian Pac.Is.

SANDOVAL Ranking: 49 *Hispanic* 287 *Overall* USA Total People: **96,303**
90.7% Hispanic **6.0%** White **0.2%** Black **2.2%** Am. Indian **0.6%** Asian Pac.Is.

GUERRERO Ranking: 50 *Hispanic* 291 *Overall* USA Total People: **94,152**
91.3% Hispanic **5.2%** White **0.3%** Black **0.3%** Am. Indian **2.4%** Asian Pac.Is.

ALVARADO Ranking: 51 *Hispanic* 294 *Overall* USA Total People: **93,723**
93.6% Hispanic **4.8%** White **0.3%** Black **0.3%** Am. Indian **0.6%** Asian Pac.Is.

ORTEGA Ranking: 52 *Hispanic* 296 *Overall* USA Total People: **93,131**
91.8% Hispanic **5.7%** White **0.3%** Black **0.6%** Am. Indian **1.1%** Asian Pac.Is.

ESTRADA Ranking: 53 *Hispanic* 298 *Overall* USA Total People: **92,831**
91.7% Hispanic **5.2%** White **0.5%** Black **0.3%** Am. Indian **1.8%** Asian Pac.Is.

CONTRERAS Ranking: 54 *Hispanic* 299 *Overall* USA Total People: **92,660**
93.8% Hispanic **4.7%** White **0.2%** Black **0.3%** Am. Indian **0.6%** Asian Pac.Is.

SANTIAGO   Ranking: **55** *Hispanic*   **302** *Overall*   USA Total People: **90,967**
87.2% Hispanic   **5.9%** White   **1.5%** Black   **0.2%** Am. Indian   **4.4%** Asian Pac.Is.

NUNEZ   Ranking: **56** *Hispanic*   **306** *Overall*   USA Total People: **90,208**
91.2% Hispanic   **6.4%** White   **0.8%** Black   **0.3%** Am. Indian   **0.8%** Asian Pac.Is.

MALDONADO   Ranking: **57** *Hispanic*   **316** *Overall*   USA Total People: **88,016**
93.0% Hispanic   **5.5%** White   **0.5%** Black   **0.3%** Am. Indian   **0.3%** Asian Pac.Is.

VEGA   Ranking: **58** *Hispanic*   **318** *Overall*   USA Total People: **87,728**
91.5% Hispanic   **6.5%** White   **0.6%** Black   **0.3%** Am. Indian   **0.7%** Asian Pac.Is.

VAZQUEZ   Ranking: **59** *Hispanic*   **328** *Overall*   USA Total People: **84,926**
94.5% Hispanic   **4.6%** White   **0.3%** Black   **0.1%** Am. Indian   **0.2%** Asian Pac.Is.

DOMINGUEZ   Ranking: **60** *Hispanic*   **334** *Overall*   USA Total People: **83,731**
91.4% Hispanic   **6.2%** White   **0.4%** Black   **0.4%** Am. Indian   **1.2%** Asian Pac.Is.

PADILLA   Ranking: **61** *Hispanic*   **345** *Overall*   USA Total People: **81,805**
89.0% Hispanic   **6.9%** White   **0.3%** Black   **1.0%** Am. Indian   **2.1%** Asian Pac.Is.

MARQUEZ   Ranking: **62** *Hispanic*   **357** *Overall*   USA Total People: **79,951**
89.8% Hispanic   **5.7%** White   **0.6%** Black   **0.5%** Am. Indian   **2.8%** Asian Pac.Is.

ESPINOZA   Ranking: **63** *Hispanic*   **360** *Overall*   USA Total People: **79,322**
94.3% Hispanic   **4.4%** White   **0.3%** Black   **0.4%** Am. Indian   **0.4%** Asian Pac.Is.

CORTEZ   Ranking: **64** *Hispanic*   **367** *Overall*   USA Total People: **77,492**
88.5% Hispanic   **7.0%** White   **0.7%** Black   **0.3%** Am. Indian   **2.8%** Asian Pac.Is.

ACOSTA   Ranking: **65** *Hispanic*   **377** *Overall*   USA Total People: **76,477**
88.0% Hispanic   **8.0%** White   **0.7%** Black   **0.3%** Am. Indian   **2.4%** Asian Pac.Is.

LUNA   Ranking: **66** *Hispanic*   **378** *Overall*   USA Total People: **76,127**
86.6% Hispanic   **9.8%** White   **0.4%** Black   **0.6%** Am. Indian   **2.0%** Asian Pac.Is.

NAVARRO   Ranking: **67** *Hispanic*   **388** *Overall*   USA Total People: **73,970**
86.6% Hispanic   **7.9%** White   **0.5%** Black   **0.3%** Am. Indian   **4.1%** Asian Pac.Is.

ROJAS   Ranking: **68** *Hispanic*   **393** *Overall*   USA Total People: **73,071**
93.3% Hispanic   **4.8%** White   **0.4%** Black   **0.2%** Am. Indian   **0.9%** Asian Pac.Is.

FIGUEROA   Ranking: **69** *Hispanic*   **398** *Overall*   USA Total People: **72,533**
91.9% Hispanic   **5.5%** White   **0.9%** Black   **0.2%** Am. Indian   **1.0%** Asian Pac.Is.

MOLINA   Ranking: **70** *Hispanic*   **417** *Overall*   USA Total People: **70,211**
89.1% Hispanic   **6.6%** White   **0.5%** Black   **0.9%** Am. Indian   **2.3%** Asian Pac.Is.

CAMPOS   Ranking: **71** *Hispanic*   **420** *Overall*   USA Total People: **69,950**
89.6% Hispanic   **7.6%** White   **0.3%** Black   **0.3%** Am. Indian   **1.5%** Asian Pac.Is.

AVILA   Ranking: **72** *Hispanic*   **421** *Overall*   USA Total People: **69,843**
89.4% Hispanic   **8.3%** White   **0.4%** Black   **0.3%** Am. Indian   **0.9%** Asian Pac.Is.

TOP 350 HISPANIC SURNAMES

JUAREZ   **Ranking: 73** *Hispanic*   **429** *Overall*   USA Total People: **68,785**
94.7% Hispanic **4.1%** White **0.2%** Black **0.2%** Am. Indian **0.4%** Asian Pac.Is.

DURAN   **Ranking: 74** *Hispanic*   **434** *Overall*   USA Total People: **68,046**
85.2% Hispanic **11.6%** White **0.6%** Black **0.9%** Am. Indian **1.1%** Asian Pac.Is.

MIRANDA   **Ranking: 75** *Hispanic*   **437** *Overall*   USA Total People: **67,646**
78.2% Hispanic **14.3%** White **1.0%** Black **0.6%** Am. Indian **4.1%** Asian Pac.Is.

CARRILLO   **Ranking: 76** *Hispanic*   **443** *Overall*   USA Total People: **67,054**
92.1% Hispanic **6.0%** White **0.3%** Black **0.5%** Am. Indian **0.7%** Asian Pac.Is.

MEJIA   **Ranking: 77** *Hispanic*   **448** *Overall*   USA Total People: **66,534**
93.3% Hispanic **4.0%** White **0.5%** Black **0.3%** Am. Indian **1.4%** Asian Pac.Is.

AYALA   **Ranking: 78** *Hispanic*   **449** *Overall*   USA Total People: **66,515**
93.5% Hispanic **4.8%** White **0.6%** Black **0.2%** Am. Indian **0.5%** Asian Pac.Is.

DELEON   **Ranking: 79** *Hispanic*   **460** *Overall*   USA Total People: **65,598**
81.9% Hispanic **7.6%** White **1.1%** Black **0.2%** Am. Indian **8.3%** Asian Pac.Is.

LEON   **Ranking: 80** *Hispanic*   **483** *Overall*   USA Total People: **62,034**
81.7% Hispanic **13.0%** White **3.0%** Black **0.5%** Am. Indian **1.2%** Asian Pac.Is.

ROBLES   **Ranking: 81** *Hispanic*   **489** *Overall*   USA Total People: **61,619**
90.6% Hispanic **5.9%** White **0.5%** Black **0.4%** Am. Indian **2.1%** Asian Pac.Is.

SALINAS   **Ranking: 82** *Hispanic*   **490** *Overall*   USA Total People: **61,582**
92.5% Hispanic **5.7%** White **0.2%** Black **0.3%** Am. Indian **1.0%** Asian Pac.Is.

SOLIS   **Ranking: 83** *Hispanic*   **497** *Overall*   USA Total People: **60,045**
91.5% Hispanic **5.9%** White **0.5%** Black **0.2%** Am. Indian **1.6%** Asian Pac.Is.

LARA   **Ranking: 84** *Hispanic*   **501** *Overall*   USA Total People: **59,731**
91.3% Hispanic **6.3%** White **0.4%** Black **0.4%** Am. Indian **1.1%** Asian Pac.Is.

TRUJILLO   **Ranking: 85** *Hispanic*   **504** *Overall*   USA Total People: **59,609**
88.1% Hispanic **9.1%** White **0.2%** Black **1.9%** Am. Indian **0.2%** Asian Pac.Is.

ROMAN   **Ranking: 86** *Hispanic*   **507** *Overall*   USA Total People: **59,020**
70.6% Hispanic **25.6%** White **2.0%** Black **0.2%** Am. Indian **0.9%** Asian Pac.Is.

AGUIRRE   **Ranking: 87** *Hispanic*   **508** *Overall*   USA Total People: **58,918**
91.5% Hispanic **6.3%** White **0.3%** Black **0.3%** Am. Indian **1.2%** Asian Pac.Is.

PACHECO   **Ranking: 88** *Hispanic*   **512** *Overall*   USA Total People: **58,534**
77.7% Hispanic **18.2%** White **0.5%** Black **0.9%** Am. Indian **1.2%** Asian Pac.Is.

CERVANTES   **Ranking: 89** *Hispanic*   **520** *Overall*   USA Total People: **57,685**
94.5% Hispanic **4.0%** White **0.1%** Black **0.3%** Am. Indian **0.9%** Asian Pac.Is.

OCHOA   **Ranking: 90** *Hispanic*   **523** *Overall*   USA Total People: **57,210**
93.2% Hispanic **5.2%** White **0.3%** Black **0.4%** Am. Indian **0.6%** Asian Pac.Is.

CABRERA   **Ranking: 91** *Hispanic*   **524** *Overall*   USA Total People: **57,171**
89.7% Hispanic   **5.5%** White   **0.5%** Black   **0.2%** Am. Indian   **3.6%** Asian Pac.Is.

VELASQUEZ   **Ranking: 92** *Hispanic*   **525** *Overall*   USA Total People: **57,163**
91.3% Hispanic   **5.3%** White   **0.6%** Black   **0.6%** Am. Indian   **1.7%** Asian Pac.Is.

MONTOYA   **Ranking: 93** *Hispanic*   **526** *Overall*   USA Total People: **57,075**
87.8% Hispanic   **8.7%** White   **0.2%** Black   **1.7%** Am. Indian   **0.8%** Asian Pac.Is.

CARDENAS   **Ranking: 94** *Hispanic*   **529** *Overall*   USA Total People: **56,618**
93.0% Hispanic   **5.1%** White   **0.3%** Black   **0.2%** Am. Indian   **1.0%** Asian Pac.Is.

FUENTES   **Ranking: 95** *Hispanic*   **530** *Overall*   USA Total People: **56,441**
91.5% Hispanic   **5.8%** White   **0.5%** Black   **0.3%** Am. Indian   **1.5%** Asian Pac.Is.

COLON   **Ranking: 96** *Hispanic*   **539** *Overall*   USA Total People: **55,512**
89.0% Hispanic   **7.9%** White   **2.1%** Black   **0.1%** Am. Indian   **0.3%** Asian Pac.Is.

SERRANO   **Ranking: 97** *Hispanic*   **545** *Overall*   USA Total People: **55,057**
89.3% Hispanic   **6.3%** White   **0.8%** Black   **0.2%** Am. Indian   **2.8%** Asian Pac.Is.

CALDERON   **Ranking: 98** *Hispanic*   **550** *Overall*   USA Total People: **54,691**
91.1% Hispanic   **5.9%** White   **0.7%** Black   **0.2%** Am. Indian   **1.7%** Asian Pac.Is.

GALLEGOS   **Ranking: 99** *Hispanic*   **551** *Overall*   USA Total People: **54,672**
89.9% Hispanic   **8.3%** White   **0.2%** Black   **0.6%** Am. Indian   **0.5%** Asian Pac.Is.

RIVAS   **Ranking: 100** *Hispanic*   **553** *Overall*   USA Total People: **54,588**
92.4% Hispanic   **5.8%** White   **0.6%** Black   **0.3%** Am. Indian   **0.4%** Asian Pac.Is.

GUERRA   **Ranking: 101** *Hispanic*   **554** *Overall*   USA Total People: **54,575**
84.9% Hispanic   **12.7%** White   **0.7%** Black   **0.6%** Am. Indian   **0.5%** Asian Pac.Is.

FRANCO   **Ranking: 102** *Hispanic*   **571** *Overall*   USA Total People: **53,161**
77.2% Hispanic   **19.3%** White   **0.6%** Black   **0.4%** Am. Indian   **1.8%** Asian Pac.Is.

ROSALES   **Ranking: 103** *Hispanic*   **595** *Overall*   USA Total People: **51,336**
92.2% Hispanic   **4.2%** White   **0.4%** Black   **0.2%** Am. Indian   **2.6%** Asian Pac.Is.

CASTANEDA   **Ranking: 104** *Hispanic*   **600** *Overall*   USA Total People: **51,089**
92.6% Hispanic   **4.5%** White   **0.2%** Black   **0.3%** Am. Indian   **2.0%** Asian Pac.Is.

TREVINO   **Ranking: 105** *Hispanic*   **612** *Overall*   USA Total People: **50,454**
91.3% Hispanic   **7.4%** White   **0.2%** Black   **0.5%** Am. Indian   **0.2%** Asian Pac.Is.

VILLARREAL   **Ranking: 106** *Hispanic*   **613** *Overall*   USA Total People: **50,351**
92.5% Hispanic   **6.6%** White   **0.2%** Black   **0.2%** Am. Indian   **0.2%** Asian Pac.Is.

VALENCIA   **Ranking: 107** *Hispanic*   **616** *Overall*   USA Total People: **50,026**
88.0% Hispanic   **5.9%** White   **0.5%** Black   **1.4%** Am. Indian   **3.6%** Asian Pac.Is.

DELACRUZ   **Ranking: 108** *Hispanic*   **629** *Overall*   USA Total People: **49,158**
74.9% Hispanic   **4.5%** White   **0.5%** Black   **0.3%** Am. Indian   **18.2%** Asian Pac.Is.

TOP 350 HISPANIC SURNAMES

CAMACHO   Ranking: 109 *Hispanic*   630 *Overall* USA Total People: **49,000**
88.4% Hispanic **7.1%** White **0.6%** Black **0.2%** Am. Indian **2.8%** Asian Pac. Is.

SALAS   Ranking: 110 *Hispanic*   643 *Overall* USA Total People: **48,282**
89.7% Hispanic **6.8%** White **0.3%** Black **0.5%** Am. Indian **2.1%** Asian Pac. Is.

SUAREZ   Ranking: 111 *Hispanic*   658 *Overall* USA Total People: **47,235**
87.3% Hispanic **9.3%** White **0.7%** Black **0.2%** Am. Indian **2.1%** Asian Pac. Is.

IBARRA   Ranking: 112 *Hispanic*   662 *Overall* USA Total People: **46,895**
94.7% Hispanic **3.2%** White **0.1%** Black **0.2%** Am. Indian **1.4%** Asian Pac. Is.

MACIAS   Ranking: 113 *Hispanic*   664 *Overall* USA Total People: **46,739**
93.6% Hispanic **5.3%** White **0.2%** Black **0.3%** Am. Indian **0.3%** Asian Pac. Is.

ANDRADE   Ranking: 114 *Hispanic*   666 *Overall* USA Total People: **46,702**
74.4% Hispanic **16.9%** White **1.7%** Black **0.3%** Am. Indian **1.7%** Asian Pac. Is.

MERCADO   Ranking: 115 *Hispanic*   674 *Overall* USA Total People: **46,437**
86.3% Hispanic **5.7%** White **0.6%** Black **0.2%** Am. Indian **6.4%** Asian Pac. Is.

ZAMORA   Ranking: 116 *Hispanic*   684 *Overall* USA Total People: **45,806**
90.5% Hispanic **6.0%** White **0.2%** Black **0.4%** Am. Indian **2.4%** Asian Pac. Is.

OROZCO   Ranking: 117 *Hispanic*   690 *Overall* USA Total People: **45,289**
95.1% Hispanic **3.9%** White **0.1%** Black **0.3%** Am. Indian **0.4%** Asian Pac. Is.

VILLANUEVA   Ranking: 118 *Hispanic*   703 *Overall* USA Total People: **44,570**
80.8% Hispanic **4.9%** White **0.4%** Black **0.2%** Am. Indian **12.5%** Asian Pac. Is.

SANTANA   Ranking: 119 *Hispanic*   710 *Overall* USA Total People: **43,875**
91.1% Hispanic **6.2%** White **1.1%** Black **0.2%** Am. Indian **0.5%** Asian Pac. Is.

VALENZUELA   Ranking: 120 *Hispanic*   711 *Overall* USA Total People: **43,770**
89.2% Hispanic **5.6%** White **0.2%** Black **2.1%** Am. Indian **2.4%** Asian Pac. Is.

BARRERA   Ranking: 121 *Hispanic*   713 *Overall* USA Total People: **43,720**
92.0% Hispanic **5.8%** White **0.2%** Black **0.2%** Am. Indian **1.3%** Asian Pac. Is.

ESCOBAR   Ranking: 122 *Hispanic*   723 *Overall* USA Total People: **42,955**
90.6% Hispanic **6.3%** White **0.5%** Black **0.3%** Am. Indian **1.8%** Asian Pac. Is.

VELEZ   Ranking: 123 *Hispanic*   727 *Overall* USA Total People: **42,820**
90.4% Hispanic **7.2%** White **1.0%** Black **0.1%** Am. Indian **0.8%** Asian Pac. Is.

LOZANO   Ranking: 124 *Hispanic*   734 *Overall* USA Total People: **42,567**
90.8% Hispanic **6.6%** White **0.3%** Black **0.3%** Am. Indian **1.7%** Asian Pac. Is.

MELENDEZ   Ranking: 125 *Hispanic*   744 *Overall* USA Total People: **42,139**
92.0% Hispanic **5.6%** White **1.0%** Black **0.3%** Am. Indian **0.5%** Asian Pac. Is.

ROCHA   Ranking: 126 *Hispanic*   744 *Overall* USA Total People: **42,139**
79.1% Hispanic **17.5%** White **0.4%** Black **0.4%** Am. Indian **0.6%** Asian Pac. Is.

RANGEL Ranking: 127 *Hispanic* 750 *Overall* USA Total People: **41,868**
92.8% Hispanic **6.1%** White **0.2%** Black **0.3%** Am. Indian **0.3%** Asian Pac. Is.

MORA Ranking: 128 *Hispanic* 759 *Overall* USA Total People: **41,348**
89.1% Hispanic **8.6%** White **0.4%** Black **0.4%** Am. Indian **1.1%** Asian Pac. Is.

ARIAS Ranking: 129 *Hispanic* 787 *Overall* USA Total People: **40,086**
92.2% Hispanic **5.8%** White **0.4%** Black **0.2%** Am. Indian **0.9%** Asian Pac. Is.

GALVAN Ranking: 130 *Hispanic* 788 *Overall* USA Total People: **40,046**
91.5% Hispanic **6.9%** White **0.2%** Black **0.4%** Am. Indian **0.6%** Asian Pac. Is.

VELAZQUEZ Ranking: 131 *Hispanic* 789 *Overall* USA Total People: **40,030**
94.9% Hispanic **4.0%** White **0.5%** Black **0.2%** Am. Indian **0.1%** Asian Pac. Is.

CANTU Ranking: 132 *Hispanic* 793 *Overall* USA Total People: **39,601**
91.0% Hispanic **7.7%** White **0.5%** Black **0.3%** Am. Indian **0.2%** Asian Pac. Is.

VILLA Ranking: 133 *Hispanic* 797 *Overall* USA Total People: **39,402**
86.3% Hispanic **10.2%** White **0.4%** Black **0.4%** Am. Indian **2.1%** Asian Pac. Is.

ZUNIGA Ranking: 134 *Hispanic* 804 *Overall* USA Total People: **39,057**
93.6% Hispanic **4.6%** White **0.4%** Black **0.3%** Am. Indian **0.8%** Asian Pac. Is.

PINEDA Ranking: 135 *Hispanic* 806 *Overall* USA Total People: **38,999**
89.2% Hispanic **4.3%** White **0.4%** Black **0.2%** Am. Indian **5.5%** Asian Pac. Is.

ACEVEDO Ranking: 136 *Hispanic* 824 *Overall* USA Total People: **38,232**
92.6% Hispanic **5.6%** White **0.7%** Black **0.2%** Am. Indian **0.4%** Asian Pac. Is.

BAUTISTA Ranking: 137 *Hispanic* 830 *Overall* USA Total People: **37,847**
71.6% Hispanic **3.8%** White **0.3%** Black **0.5%** Am. Indian **22.0%** Asian Pac. Is.

ARROYO Ranking: 138 *Hispanic* 833 *Overall* USA Total People: **37,678**
92.5% Hispanic **5.3%** White **0.7%** Black **0.2%** Am. Indian **1.0%** Asian Pac. Is.

MEZA Ranking: 139 *Hispanic* 835 *Overall* USA Total People: **37,662**
94.7% Hispanic **4.3%** White **0.3%** Black **0.3%** Am. Indian **0.2%** Asian Pac. Is.

TAPIA Ranking: 140 *Hispanic* 845 *Overall* USA Total People: **37,201**
92.9% Hispanic **5.2%** White **0.3%** Black **0.5%** Am. Indian **0.7%** Asian Pac. Is.

CISNEROS Ranking: 141 *Hispanic* 850 *Overall* USA Total People: **37,050**
94.1% Hispanic **5.0%** White **0.3%** Black **0.2%** Am. Indian **0.2%** Asian Pac. Is.

SOSA Ranking: 142 *Hispanic* 859 *Overall* USA Total People: **36,813**
92.5% Hispanic **5.8%** White **0.4%** Black **0.2%** Am. Indian **0.7%** Asian Pac. Is.

ROSARIO Ranking: 143 *Hispanic* 865 *Overall* USA Total People: **36,539**
86.8% Hispanic **6.2%** White **1.7%** Black **0.2%** Am. Indian **4.1%** Asian Pac. Is.

RUBIO Ranking: 144 *Hispanic* 866 *Overall* USA Total People: **36,531**
90.4% Hispanic **6.4%** White **0.4%** Black **0.4%** Am. Indian **1.9%** Asian Pac. Is.

TOP 350 HISPANIC SURNAMES

PONCE   **Ranking: 145** *Hispanic*   **895** *Overall*   USA Total People: **35,400**
90.7% Hispanic   **6.3%** White   **0.4%** Black   **0.2%** Am. Indian   **1.9%** Asian Pac. Is.

MONTES   **Ranking: 146** *Hispanic*   **901** *Overall*   USA Total People: **35,196**
91.8% Hispanic   **5.9%** White   **0.6%** Black   **0.4%** Am. Indian   **0.8%** Asian Pac. Is.

CORDOVA   **Ranking: 147** *Hispanic*   **903** *Overall*   USA Total People: **35,074**
85.3% Hispanic   **11.2%** White   **0.6%** Black   **0.8%** Am. Indian   **1.3%** Asian Pac. Is.

ARELLANO   **Ranking: 148** *Hispanic*   **905** *Overall*   USA Total People: **34,999**
91.2% Hispanic   **5.0%** White   **0.2%** Black   **0.3%** Am. Indian   **2.8%** Asian Pac. Is.

MATA   **Ranking: 149** *Hispanic*   **907** *Overall*   USA Total People: **34,888**
90.1% Hispanic   **6.2%** White   **0.2%** Black   **0.4%** Am. Indian   **2.4%** Asian Pac. Is.

BONILLA   **Ranking: 150** *Hispanic*   **908** *Overall*   USA Total People: **34,824**
91.8% Hispanic   **5.5%** White   **0.9%** Black   **0.2%** Am. Indian   **1.1%** Asian Pac. Is.

BELTRAN   **Ranking: 151** *Hispanic*   **914** *Overall*   USA Total People: **34,736**
89.5% Hispanic   **5.9%** White   **0.3%** Black   **0.3%** Am. Indian   **3.5%** Asian Pac. Is.

VILLEGAS   **Ranking: 152** *Hispanic*   **917** *Overall*   USA Total People: **34,684**
91.1% Hispanic   **4.5%** White   **0.3%** Black   **0.4%** Am. Indian   **3.2%** Asian Pac. Is.

DAVILA   **Ranking: 153** *Hispanic*   **924** *Overall*   USA Total People: **34,541**
91.6% Hispanic   **6.7%** White   **0.7%** Black   **0.2%** Am. Indian   **0.4%** Asian Pac. Is.

ZAVALA   **Ranking: 154** *Hispanic*   **938** *Overall*   USA Total People: **34,068**
95.1% Hispanic   **4.1%** White   **0.2%** Black   **0.2%** Am. Indian   **0.2%** Asian Pac. Is.

LUCERO   **Ranking: 155** *Hispanic*   **945** *Overall*   USA Total People: **33,922**
81.5% Hispanic   **11.9%** White   **0.2%** Black   **3.1%** Am. Indian   **2.5%** Asian Pac. Is.

BENITEZ   **Ranking: 156** *Hispanic*   **957** *Overall*   USA Total People: **33,441**
92.1% Hispanic   **5.0%** White   **0.5%** Black   **0.1%** Am. Indian   **1.8%** Asian Pac. Is.

HUERTA   **Ranking: 157** *Hispanic*   **959** *Overall*   USA Total People: **33,348**
94.6% Hispanic   **4.4%** White   **0.2%** Black   **0.2%** Am. Indian   **0.3%** Asian Pac. Is.

ESPARZA   **Ranking: 158** *Hispanic*   **971** *Overall*   USA Total People: **32,772**
93.7% Hispanic   **5.4%** White   **0.1%** Black   **0.4%** Am. Indian   **0.2%** Asian Pac. Is.

BARAJAS   **Ranking: 159** *Hispanic*   **989** *Overall*   USA Total People: **32,147**
96.0% Hispanic   **3.3%** White   **0.2%** Black   **0.2%** Am. Indian   **0.2%** Asian Pac. Is.

CUEVAS   **Ranking: 160** *Hispanic*   **993** *Overall*   USA Total People: **32,015**
88.1% Hispanic   **9.0%** White   **0.3%** Black   **0.2%** Am. Indian   **1.9%** Asian Pac. Is.

MURILLO   **Ranking: 161** *Hispanic*   **995** *Overall*   USA Total People: **31,964**
93.1% Hispanic   **4.8%** White   **0.3%** Black   **0.4%** Am. Indian   **0.9%** Asian Pac. Is.

DUARTE   **Ranking: 162** *Hispanic*   **997** *Overall*   USA Total People: **31,896**
76.6% Hispanic   **18.1%** White   **1.3%** Black   **0.3%** Am. Indian   **1.0%** Asian Pac. Is.

DEJESUS — Ranking: 163 *Hispanic* 1,002 *Overall* USA Total People: **31,803**
82.8% Hispanic **6.4%** White **1.6%** Black **0.2%** Am. Indian **7.8%** Asian Pac. Is.

MARIN — Ranking: 164 *Hispanic* 1,003 *Overall* USA Total People: **31,786**
82.6% Hispanic **14.7%** White **1.2%** Black **0.2%** Am. Indian **0.7%** Asian Pac. Is.

FELIX — Ranking: 165 *Hispanic* 1,011 *Overall* USA Total People: **31,631**
62.4% Hispanic **21.2%** White **11.2%** Black **1.0%** Am. Indian **2.6%** Asian Pac. Is.

SALGADO — Ranking: 166 *Hispanic* 1,012 *Overall* USA Total People: **31,627**
92.9% Hispanic **4.6%** White **0.3%** Black **0.4%** Am. Indian **1.4%** Asian Pac. Is.

ROSAS — Ranking: 167 *Hispanic* 1,030 *Overall* USA Total People: **31,050**
94.0% Hispanic **4.7%** White **0.2%** Black **0.2%** Am. Indian **0.5%** Asian Pac. Is.

GUEVARA — Ranking: 168 *Hispanic* 1,039 *Overall* USA Total People: **30,844**
90.4% Hispanic **5.1%** White **0.5%** Black **0.3%** Am. Indian **3.0%** Asian Pac. Is.

ESPINOSA — Ranking: 169 *Hispanic* 1,047 *Overall* USA Total People: **30,538**
86.0% Hispanic **9.1%** White **0.5%** Black **0.4%** Am. Indian **3.4%** Asian Pac. Is.

PALACIOS — Ranking: 170 *Hispanic* 1,057 *Overall* USA Total People: **30,231**
93.0% Hispanic **5.2%** White **0.5%** Black **0.2%** Am. Indian **0.7%** Asian Pac. Is.

CORTES — Ranking: 171 *Hispanic* 1,061 *Overall* USA Total People: **30,141**
86.7% Hispanic **9.0%** White **1.3%** Black **0.1%** Am. Indian **2.4%** Asian Pac. Is.

QUINTERO — Ranking: 172 *Hispanic* 1,070 *Overall* USA Total People: **29,952**
93.0% Hispanic **5.0%** White **0.4%** Black **0.9%** Am. Indian **0.3%** Asian Pac. Is.

ENRIQUEZ — Ranking: 173 *Hispanic* 1,072 *Overall* USA Total People: **29,886**
85.3% Hispanic **5.3%** White **0.6%** Black **0.4%** Am. Indian **7.8%** Asian Pac. Is.

QUINTANA — Ranking: 174 *Hispanic* 1,073 *Overall* USA Total People: **29,755**
87.3% Hispanic **9.5%** White **0.4%** Black **1.3%** Am. Indian **1.0%** Asian Pac. Is.

CORONA — Ranking: 175 *Hispanic* 1,081 *Overall* USA Total People: **29,525**
87.9% Hispanic **10.9%** White **0.2%** Black **0.2%** Am. Indian **0.3%** Asian Pac. Is.

BERNAL — Ranking: 176 *Hispanic* 1,089 *Overall* USA Total People: **29,418**
87.2% Hispanic **9.0%** White **0.6%** Black **0.4%** Am. Indian **2.2%** Asian Pac. Is.

MEDRANO — Ranking: 177 *Hispanic* 1,091 *Overall* USA Total People: **29,386**
92.4% Hispanic **4.6%** White **0.3%** Black **0.3%** Am. Indian **2.0%** Asian Pac. Is.

LUGO — Ranking: 178 *Hispanic* 1,092 *Overall* USA Total People: **29,328**
90.3% Hispanic **7.6%** White **1.0%** Black **0.4%** Am. Indian **0.3%** Asian Pac. Is.

CORREA — Ranking: 179 *Hispanic* 1,109 *Overall* USA Total People: **28,910**
84.1% Hispanic **11.0%** White **0.9%** Black **0.3%** Am. Indian **1.8%** Asian Pac. Is.

BLANCO — Ranking: 180 *Hispanic* 1,115 *Overall* USA Total People: **28,843**
79.7% Hispanic **14.6%** White **1.4%** Black **0.2%** Am. Indian **3.4%** Asian Pac. Is.

TOP 350 HISPANIC SURNAMES

ROSA   Ranking: 181 *Hispanic* 1,132 *Overall* USA Total People: **28,375**
61.3% Hispanic **32.3%**White **1.9%**Black **0.2%** Am. Indian **1.2%** Asian Pac.Is.

LEAL   Ranking: 182 *Hispanic* 1,133 *Overall* USA Total People: **28,248**
83.0% Hispanic **14.2%**White **0.6%**Black **0.3%** Am. Indian **0.9%** Asian Pac.Is.

DELAROSA   Ranking: 183 *Hispanic* 1,137 *Overall* USA Total People: **28,134**
87.8% Hispanic **5.9%** White **0.5%**Black **0.3%** Am. Indian **4.9%** Asian Pac.Is.

JARAMILLO   Ranking: 184 *Hispanic* 1,144 *Overall* USA Total People: **28,024**
89.5% Hispanic **7.8%** White **0.2%**Black **0.9%** Am. Indian **1.1%** Asian Pac.Is.

NIEVES   Ranking: 185 *Hispanic* 1,146 *Overall* USA Total People: **28,011**
91.5% Hispanic **6.2%** White **1.2%**Black **0.1%** Am. Indian **0.7%** Asian Pac.Is.

BRAVO   Ranking: 186 *Hispanic* 1,165 *Overall* USA Total People: **27,576**
88.7% Hispanic **7.8%** White **0.7%**Black **0.4%** Am. Indian **1.9%** Asian Pac.Is.

MAGANA   Ranking: 187 *Hispanic* 1,166 *Overall* USA Total People: **27,571**
94.8% Hispanic **3.8%** White **0.2%**Black **0.2%** Am. Indian **0.6%** Asian Pac.Is.

TREJO   Ranking: 188 *Hispanic* 1,172 *Overall* USA Total People: **27,383**
94.2% Hispanic **4.6%** White **0.4%**Black **0.4%** Am. Indian **0.1%** Asian Pac.Is.

QUINONES   Ranking: 189 *Hispanic* 1,177 *Overall* USA Total People: **27,290**
90.5% Hispanic **6.4%** White **1.3%**Black **0.2%** Am. Indian **1.0%** Asian Pac.Is.

REYNA   Ranking: 190 *Hispanic* 1,181 *Overall* USA Total People: **27,215**
92.4% Hispanic **6.3%** White **0.2%**Black **0.5%** Am. Indian **0.4%** Asian Pac.Is.

SAENZ   Ranking: 191 *Hispanic* 1,182 *Overall* USA Total People: **27,211**
90.9% Hispanic **7.9%** White **0.2%**Black **0.4%** Am. Indian **0.4%** Asian Pac.Is.

CANO   Ranking: 192 *Hispanic* 1,185 *Overall* USA Total People: **27,179**
90.2% Hispanic **7.7%** White **0.2%**Black **0.3%** Am. Indian **1.1%** Asian Pac.Is.

VILLALOBOS   Ranking: 193 *Hispanic* 1,188 *Overall* USA Total People: **27,107**
94.0% Hispanic **4.6%** White **0.2%**Black **0.3%** Am. Indian **0.6%** Asian Pac.Is.

VENTURA   Ranking: 194 *Hispanic* 1,196 *Overall* USA Total People: **26,769**
65.6% Hispanic **26.2%**White **0.8%**Black **0.5%** Am. Indian **5.3%** Asian Pac.Is.

GALINDO   Ranking: 195 *Hispanic* 1,199 *Overall* USA Total People: **26,730**
91.3% Hispanic **6.8%** White **0.2%**Black **0.4%** Am. Indian **0.9%** Asian Pac.Is.

PARRA   Ranking: 196 *Hispanic* 1,203 *Overall* USA Total People: **26,654**
90.9% Hispanic **7.5%** White **0.3%**Black **0.5%** Am. Indian **0.3%** Asian Pac.Is.

NAVA   Ranking: 197 *Hispanic* 1,212 *Overall* USA Total People: **26,463**
92.7% Hispanic **5.3%** White **0.2%**Black **0.2%** Am. Indian **1.1%** Asian Pac.Is.

RODRIQUEZ   Ranking: 198 *Hispanic* 1,217 *Overall* USA Total People: **26,377**
89.7% Hispanic **7.1%** White **1.7%**Black **0.6%** Am. Indian **0.3%** Asian Pac.Is.

ESQUIVEL Ranking: **199** *Hispanic* **1,220** *Overall* USA Total People: **26,301**
93.5% Hispanic **4.9%** White **0.2%** Black **0.3%** Am. Indian **0.7%** Asian Pac.Is.

VIGIL Ranking: **200** *Hispanic* **1,224** *Overall* USA Total People: **26,224**
82.0% Hispanic **13.4%** White **0.2%** Black **3.0%** Am. Indian **0.4%** Asian Pac.Is.

SIERRA Ranking: **201** *Hispanic* **1,227** *Overall* USA Total People: **26,181**
89.0% Hispanic **8.6%** White **0.9%** Black **0.5%** Am. Indian **0.5%** Asian Pac.Is.

AVALOS Ranking: **202** *Hispanic* **1,246** *Overall* USA Total People: **25,875**
95.4% Hispanic **3.8%** White **0.1%** Black **0.2%** Am. Indian **0.3%** Asian Pac.Is.

SALDANA Ranking: **203** *Hispanic* **1,273** *Overall* USA Total People: **25,386**
92.4% Hispanic **5.2%** White **0.4%** Black **0.3%** Am. Indian **1.3%** Asian Pac.Is.

PERALTA Ranking: **204** *Hispanic* **1,305** *Overall* USA Total People: **24,713**
83.3% Hispanic **6.4%** White **0.4%** Black **0.5%** Am. Indian **8.3%** Asian Pac.Is.

BACA Ranking: **205** *Hispanic* **1,316** *Overall* USA Total People: **24,572**
80.2% Hispanic **16.3%** White **0.3%** Black **2.0%** Am. Indian **0.5%** Asian Pac.Is.

VERA Ranking: **206** *Hispanic* **1,319** *Overall* USA Total People: **24,553**
89.7% Hispanic **8.2%** White **0.6%** Black **0.2%** Am. Indian **0.8%** Asian Pac.Is.

BECERRA Ranking: **207** *Hispanic* **1,325** *Overall* USA Total People: **24,468**
93.9% Hispanic **5.1%** White **0.1%** Black **0.2%** Am. Indian **0.3%** Asian Pac.Is.

CARRASCO Ranking: **208** *Hispanic* **1,331** *Overall* USA Total People: **24,343**
91.9% Hispanic **6.3%** White **0.3%** Black **0.3%** Am. Indian **0.8%** Asian Pac.Is.

MUNIZ Ranking: **209** *Hispanic* **1,340** *Overall* USA Total People: **24,203**
89.7% Hispanic **8.6%** White **0.5%** Black **0.4%** Am. Indian **0.3%** Asian Pac.Is.

ALFARO Ranking: **210** *Hispanic* **1,346** *Overall* USA Total People: **24,108**
91.8% Hispanic **5.8%** White **0.3%** Black **0.1%** Am. Indian **1.5%** Asian Pac.Is.

PORTILLO Ranking: **211** *Hispanic* **1,353** *Overall* USA Total People: **24,008**
92.7% Hispanic **5.8%** White **0.5%** Black **0.2%** Am. Indian **0.4%** Asian Pac.Is.

ZAPATA Ranking: **212** *Hispanic* **1,361** *Overall* USA Total People: **23,900**
91.9% Hispanic **5.9%** White **0.5%** Black **0.2%** Am. Indian **1.1%** Asian Pac.Is.

CARDONA Ranking: **213** *Hispanic* **1,365** *Overall* USA Total People: **23,806**
90.7% Hispanic **7.3%** White **0.4%** Black **0.1%** Am. Indian **0.9%** Asian Pac.Is.

TOVAR Ranking: **214** *Hispanic* **1,370** *Overall* USA Total People: **23,743**
93.4% Hispanic **5.4%** White **0.3%** Black **0.3%** Am. Indian **0.2%** Asian Pac.Is.

CORDERO Ranking: **215** *Hispanic* **1,409** *Overall* USA Total People: **23,127**
83.6% Hispanic **9.3%** White **0.9%** Black **0.4%** Am. Indian **5.0%** Asian Pac.Is.

VELASCO Ranking: **216** *Hispanic* **1,411** *Overall* USA Total People: **23,114**
80.1% Hispanic **7.4%** White **0.2%** Black **0.5%** Am. Indian **10.9%** Asian Pac.Is.

TOP 350 HISPANIC SURNAMES

VALLE Ranking: **217** *Hispanic* **1,415** *Overall* USA Total People: **23,039**
83.7% Hispanic **13.1%**White **0.8%**Black **0.3%** Am. Indian **1.5%** Asian Pac.Is.

BARRIOS Ranking: **218** *Hispanic* **1,427** *Overall* USA Total People: **22,941**
86.3% Hispanic **10.8%**White **0.4%**Black **0.3%** Am. Indian **1.6%** Asian Pac.Is.

SEGURA Ranking: **219** *Hispanic* **1,445** *Overall* USA Total People: **22,689**
86.8% Hispanic **10.2%**White **1.7%**Black **0.4%** Am. Indian **0.5%** Asian Pac.Is.

BAEZ Ranking: **220** *Hispanic* **1,454** *Overall* USA Total People: **22,512**
93.4% Hispanic **5.0%** White **1.0%**Black **0.1%** Am. Indian **0.2%** Asian Pac.Is.

GALLARDO Ranking: **221** *Hispanic* **1,460** *Overall* USA Total People: **22,435**
88.7% Hispanic **6.8%** White **0.1%**Black **0.2%** Am. Indian **3.4%** Asian Pac.Is.

SAUCEDO Ranking: **222** *Hispanic* **1,464** *Overall* USA Total People: **22,357**
95.2% Hispanic **3.9%** White **0.1%**Black **0.4%** Am. Indian **0.1%** Asian Pac.Is.

HURTADO Ranking: **223** *Hispanic* **1,468** *Overall* USA Total People: **22,247**
93.5% Hispanic **5.2%** White **0.3%**Black **0.4%** Am. Indian **0.3%** Asian Pac.Is.

AMAYA Ranking: **224** *Hispanic* **1,473** *Overall* USA Total People: **22,149**
93.4% Hispanic **5.2%** White **0.4%**Black **0.2%** Am. Indian **0.4%** Asian Pac.Is.

ROSADO Ranking: **225** *Hispanic* **1,479** *Overall* USA Total People: **22,066**
90.3% Hispanic **7.2%** White **1.5%**Black **0.1%** Am. Indian **0.4%** Asian Pac.Is.

ESCOBEDO Ranking: **226** *Hispanic* **1,502** *Overall* USA Total People: **21,790**
94.6% Hispanic **4.3%** White **0.1%**Black **0.3%** Am. Indian **0.4%** Asian Pac.Is.

ARREDONDO Ranking: **227** *Hispanic* **1,503** *Overall* USA Total People: **21,785**
93.8% Hispanic **5.2%** White **0.2%**Black **0.3%** Am. Indian **0.1%** Asian Pac.Is.

AGUILERA Ranking: **228** *Hispanic* **1,519** *Overall* USA Total People: **21,685**
93.5% Hispanic **5.0%** White **0.3%**Black **0.3%** Am. Indian **0.6%** Asian Pac.Is.

ZEPEDA Ranking: **229** *Hispanic* **1,545** *Overall* USA Total People: **21,305**
94.0% Hispanic **4.8%** White **0.2%**Black **0.5%** Am. Indian **0.3%** Asian Pac.Is.

GUILLEN Ranking: **230** *Hispanic* **1,550** *Overall* USA Total People: **21,257**
91.9% Hispanic **6.1%** White **0.4%**Black **0.2%** Am. Indian **1.0%** Asian Pac.Is.

HINOJOSA Ranking: **231** *Hispanic* **1,552** *Overall* USA Total People: **21,228**
93.8% Hispanic **5.4%** White **0.1%**Black **0.2%** Am. Indian **0.2%** Asian Pac.Is.

RENTERIA Ranking: **232** *Hispanic* **1,558** *Overall* USA Total People: **21,159**
94.0% Hispanic **4.7%** White **0.3%**Black **0.5%** Am. Indian **0.2%** Asian Pac.Is.

CHACON Ranking: **233** *Hispanic* **1,559** *Overall* USA Total People: **21,153**
91.2% Hispanic **7.0%** White **0.3%**Black **0.6%** Am. Indian **0.5%** Asian Pac.Is.

MONTANO Ranking: **234** *Hispanic* **1,562** *Overall* USA Total People: **21,110**
84.5% Hispanic **11.9%**White **0.5%**Black **0.8%** Am. Indian **1.6%** Asian Pac.Is.

CASTELLANOS   Ranking: **235** *Hispanic*   **1,568** *Overall*   USA Total People: **20,985**
93.9% Hispanic **5.0%** White **0.3%** Black **0.2%** Am. Indian **0.2%** Asian Pac. Is.

MADRID   Ranking: **236** *Hispanic*   **1,580** *Overall*   USA Total People: **20,834**
85.7% Hispanic **9.9%** White **0.4%** Black **0.7%** Am. Indian **2.6%** Asian Pac. Is.

ALONSO   Ranking: **237** *Hispanic*   **1,581** *Overall*   USA Total People: **20,802**
89.0% Hispanic **9.3%** White **0.2%** Black **0.2%** Am. Indian **0.9%** Asian Pac. Is.

ARAGON   Ranking: **238** *Hispanic*   **1,588** *Overall*   USA Total People: **20,723**
82.7% Hispanic **11.0%** White **0.3%** Black **2.0%** Am. Indian **3.2%** Asian Pac. Is.

PAGAN   Ranking: **239** *Hispanic*   **1,593** *Overall*   USA Total People: **20,702**
80.9% Hispanic **15.2%** White **2.4%** Black **0.1%** Am. Indian **0.7%** Asian Pac. Is.

DELATORRE   Ranking: **240** *Hispanic*   **1,600** *Overall*   USA Total People: **20,614**
91.4% Hispanic **6.0%** White **0.1%** Black **0.2%** Am. Indian **2.1%** Asian Pac. Is.

VELA   Ranking: **241** *Hispanic*   **1,603** *Overall*   USA Total People: **20,569**
91.2% Hispanic **7.5%** White **0.3%** Black **0.2%** Am. Indian **0.5%** Asian Pac. Is.

CORONADO   Ranking: **242** *Hispanic*   **1,608** *Overall*   USA Total People: **20,503**
91.9% Hispanic **5.8%** White **0.2%** Black **0.6%** Am. Indian **1.0%** Asian Pac. Is.

CABALLERO   Ranking: **243** *Hispanic*   **1,620** *Overall*   USA Total People: **20,270**
87.5% Hispanic **7.5%** White **1.0%** Black **0.3%** Am. Indian **3.1%** Asian Pac. Is.

ROMO   Ranking: **244** *Hispanic*   **1,634** *Overall*   USA Total People: **20,066**
89.1% Hispanic **9.1%** White **0.3%** Black **0.6%** Am. Indian **0.4%** Asian Pac. Is.

YBARRA   Ranking: **245** *Hispanic*   **1,639** *Overall*   USA Total People: **20,013**
88.7% Hispanic **9.6%** White **0.3%** Black **0.5%** Am. Indian **0.3%** Asian Pac. Is.

BURGOS   Ranking: **246** *Hispanic*   **1,658** *Overall*   USA Total People: **19,816**
88.7% Hispanic **6.4%** White **1.5%** Black **0.2%** Am. Indian **2.6%** Asian Pac. Is.

SERNA   Ranking: **247** *Hispanic*   **1,662** *Overall*   USA Total People: **19,751**
90.2% Hispanic **7.7%** White **0.1%** Black **0.5%** Am. Indian **1.0%** Asian Pac. Is.

VARELA   Ranking: **248** *Hispanic*   **1,664** *Overall*   USA Total People: **19,672**
88.4% Hispanic **9.0%** White **0.5%** Black **0.6%** Am. Indian **0.4%** Asian Pac. Is.

MADRIGAL   Ranking: **249** *Hispanic*   **1,672** *Overall*   USA Total People: **19,632**
92.8% Hispanic **5.4%** White **0.1%** Black **0.3%** Am. Indian **1.1%** Asian Pac. Is.

FONSECA   Ranking: **250** *Hispanic*   **1,682** *Overall*   USA Total People: **19,513**
74.6% Hispanic **19.5%** White **1.8%** Black **0.2%** Am. Indian **1.0%** Asian Pac. Is.

QUIROZ   Ranking: **251** *Hispanic*   **1,684** *Overall*   USA Total People: **19,507**
93.1% Hispanic **4.9%** White **0.2%** Black **0.4%** Am. Indian **0.8%** Asian Pac. Is.

BERMUDEZ   Ranking: **252** *Hispanic*   **1,689** *Overall*   USA Total People: **19,451**
88.5% Hispanic **6.5%** White **1.0%** Black **0.2%** Am. Indian **3.2%** Asian Pac. Is.

TOP 350 HISPANIC SURNAMES

GIL   Ranking: **253** *Hispanic* **1,691** *Overall*   USA Total People: **19,403**
84.2% Hispanic **12.4%** White **0.9%** Black **0.2%** Am. Indian **1.6%** Asian Pac. Is.

PINA   Ranking: **254** *Hispanic* **1,692** *Overall*   USA Total People: **19,399**
78.4% Hispanic **10.4%** White **3.9%** Black **0.9%** Am. Indian **0.5%** Asian Pac. Is.

CARRANZA   Ranking: **255** *Hispanic* **1,697** *Overall*   USA Total People: **19,375**
93.8% Hispanic **4.5%** White **0.3%** Black **0.2%** Am. Indian **0.9%** Asian Pac. Is.

LUJAN   Ranking: **256** *Hispanic* **1,737** *Overall*   USA Total People: **18,892**
85.5% Hispanic **9.1%** White **0.2%** Black **3.0%** Am. Indian **1.3%** Asian Pac. Is.

NIETO   Ranking: **257** *Hispanic* **1,744** *Overall*   USA Total People: **18,817**
88.6% Hispanic **8.5%** White **0.1%** Black **1.2%** Am. Indian **0.9%** Asian Pac. Is.

LEYVA   Ranking: **258** *Hispanic* **1,749** *Overall*   USA Total People: **18,769**
92.6% Hispanic **5.5%** White **0.2%** Black **0.4%** Am. Indian **0.9%** Asian Pac. Is.

RICO   Ranking: **259** *Hispanic* **1,754** *Overall*   USA Total People: **18,735**
85.9% Hispanic **10.3%** White **0.7%** Black **0.6%** Am. Indian **1.8%** Asian Pac. Is.

PAREDES   Ranking: **260** *Hispanic* **1,758** *Overall*   USA Total People: **18,689**
89.5% Hispanic **6.2%** White **0.4%** Black **0.2%** Am. Indian **3.2%** Asian Pac. Is.

BENAVIDES   Ranking: **261** *Hispanic* **1,764** *Overall*   USA Total People: **18,617**
92.3% Hispanic **6.5%** White **0.2%** Black **0.2%** Am. Indian **0.5%** Asian Pac. Is.

AVILES   Ranking: **262** *Hispanic* **1,775** *Overall*   USA Total People: **18,521**
91.8% Hispanic **5.5%** White **0.8%** Black **0.2%** Am. Indian **1.3%** Asian Pac. Is.

OLVERA   Ranking: **263** *Hispanic* **1,778** *Overall*   USA Total People: **18,512**
94.7% Hispanic **4.5%** White **0.2%** Black **0.3%** Am. Indian **0.1%** Asian Pac. Is.

AQUINO   Ranking: **264** *Hispanic* **1,781** *Overall*   USA Total People: **18,472**
50.1% Hispanic **14.9%** White **0.5%** Black **0.4%** Am. Indian **31.2%** Asian Pac. Is.

BUSTAMANTE   Ranking: **265** *Hispanic* **1,794** *Overall*   USA Total People: **18,363**
88.0% Hispanic **7.4%** White **0.3%** Black **0.5%** Am. Indian **3.1%** Asian Pac. Is.

CARMONA   Ranking: **266** *Hispanic* **1,803** *Overall*   USA Total People: **18,289**
90.5% Hispanic **7.0%** White **0.7%** Black **0.3%** Am. Indian **1.0%** Asian Pac. Is.

URIBE   Ranking: **267** *Hispanic* **1,805** *Overall*   USA Total People: **18,283**
92.7% Hispanic **6.1%** White **0.2%** Black **0.4%** Am. Indian **0.2%** Asian Pac. Is.

QUEZADA   Ranking: **268** *Hispanic* **1,820** *Overall*   USA Total People: **18,107**
95.9% Hispanic **3.1%** White **0.2%** Black **0.1%** Am. Indian **0.4%** Asian Pac. Is.

MONTALVO   Ranking: **269** *Hispanic* **1,823** *Overall*   USA Total People: **18,085**
90.3% Hispanic **8.0%** White **0.7%** Black **0.2%** Am. Indian **0.3%** Asian Pac. Is.

OSORIO   Ranking: **270** *Hispanic* **1,827** *Overall*   USA Total People: **18,037**
92.7% Hispanic **4.6%** White **0.6%** Black **0.2%** Am. Indian **1.5%** Asian Pac. Is.

YANEZ Ranking: 271 *Hispanic* 1,839 *Overall* USA Total People: 17,950
93.0% Hispanic 5.7% White 0.2% Black 0.4% Am. Indian 0.4% Asian Pac. Is.

PAZ Ranking: 272 *Hispanic* 1,858 *Overall* USA Total People: 17,776
85.7% Hispanic 9.2% White 0.3% Black 0.3% Am. Indian 3.6% Asian Pac. Is.

PRADO Ranking: 273 *Hispanic* 1,873 *Overall* USA Total People: 17,586
88.0% Hispanic 7.7% White 0.5% Black 0.2% Am. Indian 3.1% Asian Pac. Is.

CASILLAS Ranking: 274 *Hispanic* 1,882 *Overall* USA Total People: 17,498
93.3% Hispanic 5.5% White 0.3% Black 0.4% Am. Indian 0.3% Asian Pac. Is.

GRANADOS Ranking: 275 *Hispanic* 1,888 *Overall* USA Total People: 17,463
94.0% Hispanic 4.4% White 0.3% Black 0.3% Am. Indian 0.7% Asian Pac. Is.

SORIANO Ranking: 276 *Hispanic* 1,891 *Overall* USA Total People: 17,418
65.0% Hispanic 10.8% White 0.7% Black 0.3% Am. Indian 21.6% Asian Pac. Is.

ANAYA Ranking: 277 *Hispanic* 1,894 *Overall* USA Total People: 17,405
91.8% Hispanic 6.1% White 0.3% Black 0.7% Am. Indian 0.6% Asian Pac. Is.

CANALES Ranking: 278 *Hispanic* 1,897 *Overall* USA Total People: 17,381
90.8% Hispanic 7.4% White 0.7% Black 0.2% Am. Indian 0.4% Asian Pac. Is.

OCAMPO Ranking: 279 *Hispanic* 1,903 *Overall* USA Total People: 17,334
79.5% Hispanic 3.9% White 0.1% Black 0.2% Am. Indian 15.1% Asian Pac. Is.

ORNELAS Ranking: 280 *Hispanic* 1,909 *Overall* USA Total People: 17,278
92.1% Hispanic 6.6% White 0.2% Black 0.4% Am. Indian 0.3% Asian Pac. Is.

CUELLAR Ranking: 281 *Hispanic* 1,917 *Overall* USA Total People: 17,217
91.0% Hispanic 7.7% White 0.3% Black 0.3% Am. Indian 0.2% Asian Pac. Is.

FELICIANO Ranking: 282 *Hispanic* 1,933 *Overall* USA Total People: 17,112
83.9% Hispanic 8.7% White 1.1% Black 0.1% Am. Indian 5.0% Asian Pac. Is.

OTERO Ranking: 283 *Hispanic* 1,947 *Overall* USA Total People: 16,956
87.4% Hispanic 9.9% White 0.6% Black 0.9% Am. Indian 0.6% Asian Pac. Is.

SOLANO Ranking: 284 *Hispanic* 1,958 *Overall* USA Total People: 16,869
86.1% Hispanic 10.8% White 0.5% Black 0.2% Am. Indian 1.7% Asian Pac. Is.

OLIVARES Ranking: 285 *Hispanic* 1,961 *Overall* USA Total People: 16,857
93.7% Hispanic 4.6% White 0.1% Black 0.2% Am. Indian 1.0% Asian Pac. Is.

HIDALGO Ranking: 286 *Hispanic* 1,967 *Overall* USA Total People: 16,824
82.5% Hispanic 12.1% White 0.3% Black 0.2% Am. Indian 4.3% Asian Pac. Is.

MATOS Ranking: 287 *Hispanic* 1,968 *Overall* USA Total People: 16,819
79.6% Hispanic 17.1% White 1.5% Black 0.2% Am. Indian 0.3% Asian Pac. Is.

GAMEZ Ranking: 288 *Hispanic* 1,971 *Overall* USA Total People: 16,812
93.9% Hispanic 4.9% White 0.2% Black 0.3% Am. Indian 0.5% Asian Pac. Is.

TOP 350 HISPANIC SURNAMES

MARRERO Ranking: **289** *Hispanic* **1,974** *Overall* USA Total People: **16,783**
88.0% Hispanic **9.0%** White **2.0%** Black **0.1%** Am. Indian **0.4%** Asian Pac. Is.

LEMUS Ranking: **290** *Hispanic* **2,004** *Overall* USA Total People: **16,583**
93.7% Hispanic **5.0%** White **0.3%** Black **0.2%** Am. Indian **0.3%** Asian Pac. Is.

ALEMAN Ranking: **291** *Hispanic* **2,029** *Overall* USA Total People: **16,379**
90.4% Hispanic **8.3%** White **0.5%** Black **0.1%** Am. Indian **0.4%** Asian Pac. Is.

ALONZO Ranking: **292** *Hispanic* **2,038** *Overall* USA Total People: **16,326**
77.7% Hispanic **12.1%** White **2.4%** Black **1.0%** Am. Indian **5.8%** Asian Pac. Is.

REYNOSO Ranking: **293** *Hispanic* **2,049** *Overall* USA Total People: **16,208**
93.6% Hispanic **4.0%** White **0.3%** Black **0.2%** Am. Indian **1.7%** Asian Pac. Is.

OLIVAS Ranking: **294** *Hispanic* **2,053** *Overall* USA Total People: **16,164**
90.8% Hispanic **6.7%** White **0.3%** Black **0.6%** Am. Indian **1.1%** Asian Pac. Is.

VALADEZ Ranking: **295** *Hispanic* **2,064** *Overall* USA Total People: **16,083**
94.0% Hispanic **5.1%** White **0.1%** Black **0.3%** Am. Indian **0.2%** Asian Pac. Is.

BARRAGAN Ranking: **296** *Hispanic* **2,078** *Overall* USA Total People: **16,021**
95.2% Hispanic **4.2%** White **0.1%** Black **0.2%** Am. Indian **0.1%** Asian Pac. Is.

NAVARRETE Ranking: **297** *Hispanic* **2,080** *Overall* USA Total People: **16,010**
93.3% Hispanic **3.9%** White **0.2%** Black **0.1%** Am. Indian **2.1%** Asian Pac. Is.

AMADOR Ranking: **298** *Hispanic* **2,081** *Overall* USA Total People: **15,997**
87.5% Hispanic **9.6%** White **0.3%** Black **0.4%** Am. Indian **1.5%** Asian Pac. Is.

AREVALO Ranking: **299** *Hispanic* **2,087** *Overall* USA Total People: **15,942**
91.6% Hispanic **4.3%** White **0.3%** Black **0.2%** Am. Indian **3.3%** Asian Pac. Is.

BETANCOURT Ranking: **300** *Hispanic* **2,098** *Overall* USA Total People: **15,876**
88.6% Hispanic **9.6%** White **1.0%** Black **0.3%** Am. Indian **0.2%** Asian Pac. Is.

QUINTANILLA Ranking: **301** *Hispanic* **2,102** *Overall* USA Total People: **15,849**
91.8% Hispanic **5.0%** White **0.4%** Black **0.2%** Am. Indian **1.9%** Asian Pac. Is.

OJEDA Ranking: **302** *Hispanic* **2,110** *Overall* USA Total People: **15,780**
92.5% Hispanic **5.6%** White **0.5%** Black **0.2%** Am. Indian **0.9%** Asian Pac. Is.

SEPULVEDA Ranking: **303** *Hispanic* **2,131** *Overall* USA Total People: **15,611**
90.6% Hispanic **8.1%** White **0.3%** Black **0.3%** Am. Indian **0.4%** Asian Pac. Is.

VALDES Ranking: **304** *Hispanic* **2,139** *Overall* USA Total People: **15,567**
85.6% Hispanic **12.1%** White **0.7%** Black **0.1%** Am. Indian **1.0%** Asian Pac. Is.

RENDON Ranking: **305** *Hispanic* **2,165** *Overall* USA Total People: **15,375**
89.6% Hispanic **8.4%** White **0.3%** Black **0.4%** Am. Indian **0.7%** Asian Pac. Is.

TELLEZ Ranking: **306** *Hispanic* **2,174** *Overall* USA Total People: **15,320**
93.6% Hispanic **5.4%** White **0.1%** Black **0.3%** Am. Indian **0.2%** Asian Pac. Is.

SOTELO Ranking: 307 *Hispanic* 2,177 *Overall* USA Total People: **15,308**
91.2% Hispanic **5.6%** White **0.2%** Black **0.4%** Am. Indian **1.9%** Asian Pac. Is.

ESCAMILLA Ranking: 308 *Hispanic* 2,183 *Overall* USA Total People: **15,278**
94.3% Hispanic **4.5%** White **0.2%** Black **0.3%** Am. Indian **0.4%** Asian Pac. Is.

GAMBOA Ranking: 309 *Hispanic* 2,205 *Overall* USA Total People: **15,117**
83.1% Hispanic **7.2%** White **1.0%** Black **0.3%** Am. Indian **7.2%** Asian Pac. Is.

NEGRON Ranking: 310 *Hispanic* 2,208 *Overall* USA Total People: **15,090**
90.9% Hispanic **7.2%** White **1.1%** Black **0.1%** Am. Indian **0.2%** Asian Pac. Is.

LEDESMA Ranking: 311 *Hispanic* 2,211 *Overall* USA Total People: **15,077**
87.3% Hispanic **7.6%** White **0.3%** Black **0.4%** Am. Indian **3.7%** Asian Pac. Is.

CARBAJAL Ranking: 312 *Hispanic* 2,224 *Overall* USA Total People: **14,993**
93.8% Hispanic **4.4%** White **0.5%** Black **0.3%** Am. Indian **0.8%** Asian Pac. Is.

ORELLANA Ranking: 313 *Hispanic* 2,229 *Overall* USA Total People: **14,943**
94.3% Hispanic **4.4%** White **0.4%** Black **0.1%** Am. Indian **0.3%** Asian Pac. Is.

PATINO Ranking: 314 *Hispanic* 2,233 *Overall* USA Total People: **14,929**
90.5% Hispanic **7.9%** White **0.2%** Black **0.1%** Am. Indian **0.9%** Asian Pac. Is.

TORREZ Ranking: 315 *Hispanic* 2,236 *Overall* USA Total People: **14,904**
90.3% Hispanic **7.7%** White **0.5%** Black **0.8%** Am. Indian **0.2%** Asian Pac. Is.

OLIVA Ranking: 316 *Hispanic* 2,241 *Overall* USA Total People: **14,892**
66.8% Hispanic **28.5%** White **0.6%** Black **0.1%** Am. Indian **3.2%** Asian Pac. Is.

ARREOLA Ranking: 317 *Hispanic* 2,245 *Overall* USA Total People: **14,874**
94.6% Hispanic **2.6%** White **0.2%** Black **0.2%** Am. Indian **2.0%** Asian Pac. Is.

ARCE Ranking: 318 *Hispanic* 2,249 *Overall* USA Total People: **14,855**
85.9% Hispanic **8.1%** White **0.8%** Black **0.3%** Am. Indian **4.1%** Asian Pac. Is.

LONGORIA Ranking: 319 *Hispanic* 2,251 *Overall* USA Total People: **14,843**
89.5% Hispanic **9.4%** White **0.3%** Black **0.2%** Am. Indian **0.2%** Asian Pac. Is.

PRIETO Ranking: 320 *Hispanic* 2,259 *Overall* USA Total People: **14,786**
88.4% Hispanic **8.6%** White **0.5%** Black **0.4%** Am. Indian **1.6%** Asian Pac. Is.

BRITO Ranking: 321 *Hispanic* 2,262 *Overall* USA Total People: **14,740**
83.8% Hispanic **10.3%** White **1.8%** Black **0.2%** Am. Indian **0.7%** Asian Pac. Is.

VALENTIN Ranking: 322 *Hispanic* 2,265 *Overall* USA Total People: **14,720**
84.6% Hispanic **9.7%** White **3.1%** Black **0.1%** Am. Indian **1.6%** Asian Pac. Is.

ARANDA Ranking: 323 *Hispanic* 2,268 *Overall* USA Total People: **14,683**
89.1% Hispanic **7.1%** White **0.5%** Black **0.3%** Am. Indian **2.5%** Asian Pac. Is.

VENEGAS Ranking: 324 *Hispanic* 2,271 *Overall* USA Total People: **14,677**
93.9% Hispanic **4.7%** White **0.2%** Black **0.4%** Am. Indian **0.6%** Asian Pac. Is.

TOP 350 HISPANIC SURNAMES

CASAS Ranking: **325** *Hispanic* **2,275** *Overall* USA Total People: **14,635**
91.4% Hispanic **6.6%** White **0.1%** Black **0.1%** Am. Indian **1.4%** Asian Pac.Is.

CAVAZOS Ranking: **326** *Hispanic* **2,290** *Overall* USA Total People: **14,543**
92.8% Hispanic **6.5%** White **0.2%** Black **0.1%** Am. Indian **0.1%** Asian Pac.Is.

TOLEDO Ranking: **327** *Hispanic* **2,294** *Overall* USA Total People: **14,514**
73.9% Hispanic **9.7%** White **0.5%** Black **8.3%** Am. Indian **6.0%** Asian Pac.Is.

VALLEJO Ranking: **328** *Hispanic* **2,296** *Overall* USA Total People: **14,484**
90.3% Hispanic **6.6%** White **0.4%** Black **0.3%** Am. Indian **1.9%** Asian Pac.Is.

PALMA Ranking: **329** *Hispanic* **2,312** *Overall* USA Total People: **14,339**
64.9% Hispanic **27.2%** White **1.0%** Black **0.3%** Am. Indian **5.7%** Asian Pac.Is.

GALVEZ Ranking: **330** *Hispanic* **2,314** *Overall* USA Total People: **14,311**
86.4% Hispanic **5.4%** White **0.5%** Black **0.3%** Am. Indian **6.5%** Asian Pac.Is.

MENA Ranking: **331** *Hispanic* **2,317** *Overall* USA Total People: **14,299**
89.2% Hispanic **8.3%** White **0.9%** Black **0.2%** Am. Indian **0.7%** Asian Pac.Is.

BANUELOS Ranking: **332** *Hispanic* **2,326** *Overall* USA Total People: **14,260**
95.9% Hispanic **3.3%** White **0.1%** Black **0.3%** Am. Indian **0.2%** Asian Pac.Is.

ALANIZ Ranking: **333** *Hispanic* **2,341** *Overall* USA Total People: **14,169**
92.8% Hispanic **6.5%** White **0.2%** Black **0.2%** Am. Indian **0.1%** Asian Pac.Is.

GODINEZ Ranking: **334** *Hispanic* **2,346** *Overall* USA Total People: **14,152**
94.4% Hispanic **4.4%** White **0.1%** Black **0.2%** Am. Indian **0.7%** Asian Pac.Is.

PULIDO Ranking: **335** *Hispanic* **2,347** *Overall* USA Total People: **14,151**
90.3% Hispanic **4.9%** White **0.2%** Black **0.2%** Am. Indian **3.9%** Asian Pac.Is.

ESCALANTE Ranking: **336** *Hispanic* **2,365** *Overall* USA Total People: **14,032**
88.9% Hispanic **6.4%** White **0.5%** Black **1.5%** Am. Indian **1.8%** Asian Pac.Is.

ZARATE Ranking: **337** *Hispanic* **2,371** *Overall* USA Total People: **14,000**
92.1% Hispanic **4.8%** White **0.2%** Black **0.2%** Am. Indian **2.3%** Asian Pac.Is.

POLANCO Ranking: **338** *Hispanic* **2,383** *Overall* USA Total People: **13,938**
93.5% Hispanic **4.6%** White **0.7%** Black **0.3%** Am. Indian **0.5%** Asian Pac.Is.

VIDAL Ranking: **339** *Hispanic* **2,395** *Overall* USA Total People: **13,867**
75.8% Hispanic **16.6%** White **2.5%** Black **0.1%** Am. Indian **3.9%** Asian Pac.Is.

CRESPO Ranking: **340** *Hispanic* **2,401** *Overall* USA Total People: **13,835**
86.6% Hispanic **10.7%** White **1.1%** Black **0.1%** Am. Indian **0.9%** Asian Pac.Is.

DELOSSANTOS Ranking: **341** *Hispanic* **2,409** *Overall* USA Total People: **13,802**
77.9% Hispanic **4.9%** White **0.3%** Black **0.2%** Am. Indian **15.3%** Asian Pac.Is.

SALCEDO Ranking: **342** *Hispanic* **2,440** *Overall* USA Total People: **13,593**
87.7% Hispanic **5.8%** White **0.4%** Black **0.3%** Am. Indian **5.1%** Asian Pac.Is.

MOYA   Ranking: **343** *Hispanic*   **2,451** *Overall*   USA Total People: **13,526**
             87.9% Hispanic **8.2%** White **0.7%**Black **0.4%** Am. Indian **2.3%** Asian Pac.Is.

BARBOSA   Ranking: **344** *Hispanic*   **2,462** *Overall*   USA Total People: **13,433**
             64.8% Hispanic **23.1%**White **2.3%**Black **0.1%** Am. Indian **1.4%** Asian Pac.Is.

BARRAZA   Ranking: **345** *Hispanic*   **2,463** *Overall*   USA Total People: **13,430**
             95.0% Hispanic **4.2%** White **0.1%**Black **0.3%** Am. Indian **0.3%** Asian Pac.Is.

CHAPA   Ranking: **346** *Hispanic*   **2,475** *Overall*   USA Total People: **13,370**
             90.0% Hispanic **8.4%** White **0.2%**Black **0.2%** Am. Indian **0.9%** Asian Pac.Is.

SAAVEDRA   Ranking: **347** *Hispanic*   **2,479** *Overall*   USA Total People: **13,358**
             90.3% Hispanic **6.5%** White **0.2%**Black **0.5%** Am. Indian **2.0%** Asian Pac.Is.

CORRAL   Ranking: **348** *Hispanic*   **2,493** *Overall*   USA Total People: **13,252**
             91.1% Hispanic **7.1%** White **0.4%**Black **0.3%** Am. Indian **0.8%** Asian Pac.Is.

ZARAGOZA   Ranking: **349** *Hispanic*   **2,495** *Overall*   USA Total People: **13,245**
             92.6% Hispanic **4.3%** White **0.2%**Black **0.2%** Am. Indian **2.1%** Asian Pac.Is.

CERDA   Ranking: **350** *Hispanic*   **2,505** *Overall*   USA Total People: **13,215**
             93.4% Hispanic **5.6%** White **0.2%**Black **0.3%** Am. Indian **0.3%** Asian Pac.Is.

Nava's home town church in Tepetongo, Mexico

TOP 350 HISPANIC SURNAMES

*Dr. Julian Nava during his days on the Los Angeles Unified
School District Board between 1967 and 1979.*

ABOUT THE AUTHOR

AMBASSADOR JULIAN NAVA

Julian Nava has three children all in the field of education like him. His six grandchildren and wife Patricia of 49 years are the center of his life. While a lover of classical music, especially Mozart, his sweetest sound is a grandchild calling out, "granpa."

Nava is one of eight children born of parents that fled Zacatecas when the Mexican Revolution tore their region apart. The border was open then because Mexican labor was needed. The Great Depression of the 1930's changed all that and the federal government set up the Relocation Program to expel several hundred thousand Mexican workers.

The Navas and their eight children born in the U.S. were on the way to the train depot in Los Angeles when seven-year-old Julian became ill. Fortunately the family stopped at the nearby public hospital to check on him, for the next train stop would be in Phoenix 5 hours away. Within 30 minutes he was operated for a ruptured appendix. The Navas went back to the East Los Angeles barrio broken financially.

Like millions of others the Navas survived on federal relief food and faithfully studied in keeping with their father's standards—they were poor in money but rich in family solidarity. Above all, they were loyal Americans, in spite of the relocation effort. After Pearl Harbor three Nava sons in turn volunteered into the armed forces. Julian earned his Navy wings just as the war ended. That's where Julian learned to travel and became fully American while proud of his Mexican heritage.

After the war Julian became one of a new G.I. Generation that demanded being called Mexican-American, not just Mexican. Active in politics since Truman's election in 1948, in time he was to run for public office himself, becoming the first Mexican American elected to the county-wide Los Angeles School district in 1967 for twelve years. By now he was a Professor of History at Cal. State University, Northridge, from where he retired after 43 years. Unsolicited, President Jimmy Carter named him ambassador to Mexico in 1979.

By the end of his professional career he had traveled to Venezuela, Patagonia, Siberia, China, Tibet, and his favorite Spain. Various international projects have included books to found the new national library in Estonia after Russia departed. After publishing numerous books on history for schools and college, time forced him to give up skiing and tennis. However, new interests sprang up. He has enjoyed producing professional TV documentaries on the Basques, Castro's Cuba and

Mexican Immigration. A novel on Tibet is well underway alongside the manuals for writing family history. Appreciation for his family history and the strength it has given him may help explain the work before us.

Ambassador Julian Nava presenting credentials to Mexican President Jose Lopez Portillo in 1979.

The Islands Where the Moon is Born
An Adventure in the Galapagos Islands
Edna Iturralde

WPR BOOKS
PARA LOS NIÑOS

Calling Him Dad
The Summer My Father Appeared Out Of Nowhere
Virginia Kamhi

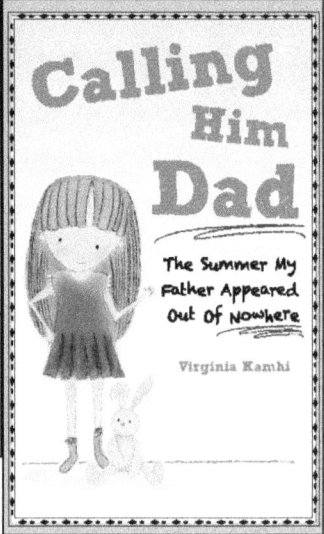

FOR OUR YOUTH FROM OUR PARA LOS NIÑOS IMPRINT

The Realities of Living in the 21st Century Series is designed to help youth better understand and appreciate the social, health and political issues that many youth face

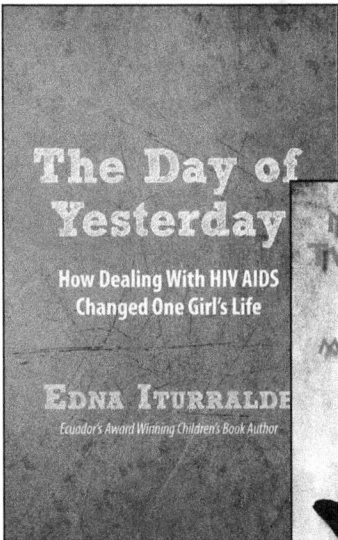

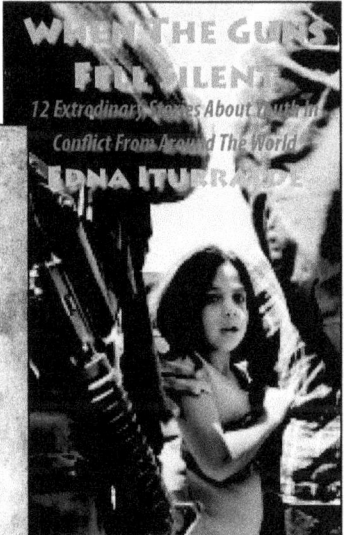

The Day of Yesterday
How Dealing With HIV AIDS Changed One Girl's Life
EDNA ITURRALDE
Ecuador's Award Winning Children's Book Author

NEGLECTED BY TWO COUNTRIES
The Rebirth of the American Dream
MARIE ELENA CORTES
SPECIAL INTRODUCTION BY AMBASSADOR JULIAN NAVA

WHEN THE GUNS FELL SILENT
12 Extraordinary Stories About Youth in Conflict From Around The World
EDNA ITURRALDE

We're adding more books every month

www.ingramcontent.com/pod-product-compliance
Lightning Source LLC
Chambersburg PA
CBHW072143020426
42334CB00018B/1872